# Praise for This Book:

"I love a book with the thesis in the title and proof of the thesis in the text. Every parent, and every couple, should read this book to prevent them from having an affair with their child(ren). What misery and suffering for all concerned, for generations to come, when couples put their marriage anywhere but first. A must-read."

— **Harville Hendrix, Ph.D.**, author of *Getting the Love You Want* and *Giving the Love That Heals: A Guide for Parents*

"As a pediatrician and pain physician, I see many children suffer due to the stress of covert marital discord. When spouses distance from each other they sometimes make their child the center of their lives, which interferes with the natural weaning process essential to healthy development. The best gift you can give your kids is to create a good marriage. David Code, in a step-wise approach, identifies and addresses how one, in a very practical way, can improve their marriage and, thus, the entire family. I recommend his book most highly."

— **David D. Sherry, M.D.**, Professor of Pediatrics at the University of Pennsylvania Medical School and the Children's Hospital of Philadelphia (ranked #1 in the U.S.)

"Stress has become a pervasive problem for couples struggling to balance the hectic lives of their kids with their own demanding jobs. David Code provides powerful preventive medicine that 'inoculates' spouses who are currently doing well, but can ben~~~ ~~~ning advice."

r of *Newsday*

"David Code is a big-picture thinker who offers preventive medicine for the American family. He has a gift for translating scientific facts into practical solutions, and his new solutions to common family problems can help solidify your marriage and improve your parenting. You will never look at your family's problems the same way again. This is a powerful contribution towards a new understanding of human behavior in families."

— **Jaak Panksepp, Ph.D.**, Distinguished Research Professor Emeritus of Psychology, Bowling Green State University; Head of Affective Neuroscience Research, Falk Center for Molecular Therapeutics, Northwestern University; and author of *Affective Neuroscience*

"David Code's book provides a win-win solution for the challenges facing today's families. Code makes a compelling argument that putting your marriage first benefits both parents and their children. He explains why good marriages produce good kids, and provides helpful advice for building a strong marriage. I hope his book enjoys a wide readership."

— **Glenn Firebaugh, Ph.D.**, Distinguished Professor of Sociology, Penn State University; Former editor, *American Sociological Review*

"Most surgeons across the country today find that over percent of our patients are taking some type of anti-anxiety drug. David Code offers a brilliant analysis of why we develop anxiety, and how anxiety affects both our marriage and our ability to raise psychologically healthy children. I highly recommend this book."

— **James W. Serene, M.D.**, Orthopaedic Surgeon and Assistant Professor at Penn State Medical School

"David Code offers a game-changing combination of Bowen family systems theory, brain research, and studies on animal instincts, to help us understand why humans do what we do in families. You'll be glad you read this book."

— Peter Titelman, Ph.D., clinical psychologist, editor of *Triangles: Bowen Family Systems Theory Perspectives,* and *Emotional Cutoff*

"In my career as a physician it became clear to me that, too often, couples lost the notion that their marriages needed nurturing in order to stay healthy. Among my peers and patients I saw families fall apart because no one paid attention to the marriage, the union that started the family. David Code's book shows us why we need to put our marriages first and then shows us how. Everyone who is balancing marriage, parenthood, and modern life should read this book."

— Mary Bruce McKenzie Serene, M.D., Board Certified Anesthesiologist, Medical School Wake Forest University School of Medicine, Residency Emory University and Grady Hospital, Atlanta Georgia

# To Raise Happy Kids, Put Your Marriage First

## DAVID CODE

*A Crossroad Book*
The Crossroad Publishing Company
New York

The Crossroad Publishing Company
www.CrossroadPublishing.com

All stories in this book come from the experiences of actual families. People's names and details of the stories have been changed to protect their privacy.

In continuation of our 200-year tradition of independent publishing, The Crossroad Publishing Company proudly offers a variety of books with strong, original voices and diverse perspectives. The viewpoints expressed in our books are not necessarily those of The Crossroad Publishing Company, any of its imprints, or of its employees. No claims are made or responsibility assumed for any health or other benefit.

Printed in the United States of America.

The text of this book is set in 11/15 Apollo. The display face is Helvetica.

Cataloging-in-Publication Data is available from the Library of Congress.

ISBN-10: 0-8245-2538-8
ISBN-13: 978-08245-2538-5

1   2   3   4   5   6   7   8   9   10          14   13   12   11   10   09

# Contents

Acknowledgments . . . . . . . . . . . . . . . . . . . . . . . . . . xi

Introduction
Three Myths That Are Harming Our Families . . . . . . . 1

*Out of the Chaos Patterns Emerge ♦ Learning from Other People's Mistakes ♦ Couples Living in Emotional Divorce ♦ Taking Stock of Your Family ♦ Myth #1: The More Attention We Give Our Kids, The Better They'll Turn Out ♦ How You Relate to Your Spouse ♦ Myth #2: Arguing Leads to Divorce ♦ How You View Your Marriage ♦ Myth #3: If We Feel Unfulfilled in Our Marriage, It's Because We Married the Wrong Person ♦ Just One Degree of Change Alters the Rest of Your Life*

## PART 1
## HOW WE HURT OUR KIDS
## WITHOUT REALIZING IT

1 How We Create a Self-Fulfilling Prophecy
in Our Kids . . . . . . . . . . . . . . . . . . . . . . . . . . . . . . 16

*When It Comes to Attention, Less Is More ♦ Couples Who Live Like Roommates Harm Their Kids ♦ How We Pass On Our Baggage ♦ The Four Steps of Projection onto Our Children ♦ Nature versus Nurture ♦ The Mind-Body Connection: Our Minds Affect Our Kids' Bodies ♦ Projection Summarized ♦ Your Child Is Not Your Best Friend ♦ A Wake-Up Call*

2   Why We Kill Our Kids with Kindness . . . . . . . . 44

*How versus Why* ✦ *Like All Animals, Humans Wean Their Offspring* ✦ *The Mother-Infant Bond: Ensuring Her Infant Will Thrive* ✦ *Attunement: A Conversation between Caregiver and Child* ✦ *Weaning: A Crucial Step for a Child's Independence* ✦ *How Caregiver and Child Become "Addicted" to Each Other* ✦ *Attunement: The Messenger of Escalating Anxiety* ✦ *Our Brain's Amygdala: Once-Bitten, Twice-Shy* ✦ *The Child Replays This Drama as an Adult* ✦ *Summary*

# PART 2
# HOW WE HURT OUR MARRIAGES, WHICH HURTS OUR KIDS

3   Why We Hurt Those We Love Most . . . . . . . . . . 78

*We Don't Realize We're "Trigger-Happy"* ✦ *Scapegoating: Spraying Our Anxiety onto Others* ✦ *Blamers and Self-Blamers* ✦ *A Common Pattern Leading to a Troubled Spouse or Child* ✦ *Less Drama, More Control*

4   The Silent Killer of Marriage . . . . . . . . . . . . . . 100

*The "Flight" in Our Fight-or-Flight Response* ✦ *Avoiding Our Spouse Is Worse Than Arguing* ✦ *Common Ways We Distance without Realizing It*

5   Anxiety: The Cause of Drama
in Relationships . . . . . . . . . . . . . . . . . . . . . . . 115

*What We Call "Stress" Is Actually Our Own Inner Anxiety* ✦ *A Nervous Soldier on Guard Duty* ✦ *Is It a Jungle Out There?* ✦ *Programmed to Overreact* ✦ *Imprinting: How We Pass Our Baggage On to Our Kids* ✦ *Anxiety Spreads*

Quickly through the "Herd" ✦ Incomplete Weaning versus
Imprinting ✦ Kids Pick Up On Everything: Mirror Neurons
✦ Seeing the Vicious Cycle of Anxiety ✦ Relief from Anxiety:
Self-Awareness

# PART 3
# THE SOLUTION: TO RAISE HAPPY KIDS,
# PUT YOUR MARRIAGE FIRST

6  The Grass Is Not Greener: You've Already
   Chosen Your Ideal Mate . . . . . . . . . . . . . . . . . . 144

   *Chemistry: A Primal Instinct between Mates ✦ Similar
   Levels of Anxiety ✦ Our Startle Reflex ✦ What Brings Us
   Together Also Drives Us Apart ✦ Chemistry Doesn't Lie, So
   Accept Your Mate ✦ Playing the Hand We Were Dealt*

7  Take a Crash Course on Your Family's History
   So You Don't Repeat It . . . . . . . . . . . . . . . . . . . 162

   *Benefit #1: Accepting Your Loved Ones ✦ Benefit #2:
   Improving Your Personality ✦ Let's Go on Safari! ✦ Bene-
   fit #3: Improving Your Marriage by Working with Your
   Parents ✦ The Joy of Observing Yourself ✦ I Want Inner
   Peace Now!*

8  Look for the Problem in Yourself First . . . . . . . 193

   *Step 1: Define Your Kid's Problem, and Search for That
   Same Problem within Yourself ✦ Step 2: Trace Your Kid's
   Problem Back to Its Roots in Your Family of Origin ✦ Step 3:
   View Your Child's Problem as a Sign of Anxiety in You or
   Your Marriage ✦ If You Feel Guilty, Read This ✦ Step 4:
   Recognize More of Your Own Drama So That You Will Be
   Less Anxious and Thus Pass Less Baggage On to Your Child
   ✦ Summary: Avoiding the Self-Fulfilling Prophecy*

9   We Get So Much Good Advice, But Why Can't
    We Follow Through? ..................... 216

*"Helping" Is Actually Hurting* ◆ *How to Reduce Your Worry
about What Others Think of You* ◆ *Playing Detective and
Solving Family Mysteries* ◆ *Reunion: Bringing the Demons
Out of the Closet* ◆ *The Pay-Off* ◆ *What True Compassion
Means* ◆ *Writing Out What You Believe* ◆ *Want Happy
Kids? Get a Life Yourself!* ◆ *Message to Working Mothers:
You Go, Girl!*

10  Eat, Walk, and Talk Your Way to a Happier
    Family ................................. 246

*Creating a Lifelong Friendship with Your Spouse* ◆ *Bringing
Life to Mealtimes* ◆ *The Shortcut to Marital Bliss: Visit
Your Parents* ◆ *Where Do We Go from Here?*

Notes ...................................... 261

# Acknowledgments

Like many writers, I am struck by the irony of my name alone listed on the cover as author. I'd like to acknowledge some of my "co-authors," without whom I could not have created this work.

The following people believed in me long before this book became a reality: Alexis Rizzuto, Chuck and Bonnie Rampone, Diane Debrovner, Jim and Brucie Serene, Katherine Johnson Armstrong, Kelly Bozanic, Lew Logan, Ross Garber, Lisa Marber, Victor Romero, Jose Arroyo, Linda Konner, Ron Roel, John Carey, and Tammi Hawke.

These people gave me valuable support and guidance once I was underway: David Sherry, Amy Marshall, Barbara Fontana, Bill Grimes, Bruce and Kevin Lockerbie, Christine Bell, Christine Cipriani, Paul Schneider, Len Bilello, Craig Wilson, David Janssen, Douglas and Kimberly McKenna, Geoff Shandler, Gerald McKelvey, Glenn Firebaugh, Kevin McGarry, Peter Levine, Sally Willcox, Keith Elkin, and Tim Leslie.

These people are my mentors, who have stood beside me through thick and thin: Jamie Callaway, Kathleen Kerr, Lloyd Prator, Roberta Gilbert, Robert Laird, Ward Ewing, Larry Hofer, Andy Luke, Mike Peters, George Werner, Masaro Miyajima, and Ric Connors.

These people saw the potential of my project, and they helped bring it to fruition: Gwendolin Herder, Jaak Panksepp,

Edmund Phelps, Ella Smith Kenney, John Fine, Harville Hendrix, Josh Burek, Loring Knoblauch, Charles Forelle, Marie Reilly, Elisabeth Malzahn, John Jones, Jenna Fisher, Kristin Black, Sam Waterston, and Strand Conover.

I want to thank my mom for giving me the gift of life.

My wife is not only my inspiration and the "Lennon" of our Lennon & McCartney creative duo. She is also the greatest gift God has given me.

# Introduction

# Three Myths
# That Are Harming Our Families

My father was a farmer, and so was his father. I was born on a dusty farm under the big sky of the Canadian prairie. The tap water in our house ran brown because the dust from the fields permeated everything, so we used to drive six miles every week to get clean drinking water.

As the youngest of seven children, you might say I've always been a student of family dynamics. It didn't take a village to raise us — we *were* a village. Our nearest neighbor lived over a mile away, the nearest school was thirteen miles away, and during winter the temperature could reach fifty degrees below zero. So in that big farmhouse on the barren plains of Saskatchewan, we made our own community. I remember one Christmas vacation when my older brothers and sisters returned home with their partners and children, and we had nineteen people staying in our house with only one bathroom.

I grew up loving books, music, and travel, which eventually carried me from the waving wheat fields of my childhood to the ivy-covered halls of Yale, where I began my formal study of families and community.

My fascination with families has now taken me to over fifty different cultures around the globe, where I've stayed

1

with families in fifteen countries on four continents. I learned Japanese, Russian, and French so I could explore these exotic kingdoms, watch the people living their lives, and understand their stories in their own tongue. People open up to me because I'm fascinated by them, and in my travels folks from all over the world have invited me into the inner sanctum of their families as a friend and confidant.

From this privileged vantage point, I could notice patterns in the family dynamics of other cultures. I've joined a family eating spicy morsels of snake in a tiny apartment in Shanghai and attended a Russian-Jewish funeral in Moscow. I've worried with an Indian couple over their daughter's marriage and picked dates with families on a windy desert farm in Israel. Everywhere I went, couples still loved, parents still worried, and children still wanted to make their parents proud.

But I didn't realize I was traveling around the world to discover my own back yard.

Living abroad for six years forced me to step outside my own culture, but when my brother died of AIDS and my dad died of cancer, all my years of observing other people's families suddenly bore fruit in a most surprising way. For the first time, I realized that I could now observe American families through a foreigner's eyes.

As part of my own grieving process, I began to volunteer with the families of AIDS patients and cancer victims at a local hospice. A fish does not notice the water in which it swims, but my years as a fish out of water in other countries gave me an outsider's perspective on the turbulent emotional waters in which American families swim every day. As these families invited me into the hushed rooms of their suffering, I began to see patterns I had never noticed before.

## Out of the Chaos Patterns Emerge

I noticed that families in crisis had certain characteristics in common, like blaming or avoiding each other. At first I assumed, as most people do, that the crisis in the family had caused these behaviors. As I went deeper into a family's history, however, I realized that it was actually their blaming and avoiding each other that helped *create* the crisis, not the other way around.

Then suddenly, I began to notice these same patterns in ordinary families who were not in crisis — not *yet*. It was as if I had become a fortune teller, able to predict the trouble that lay ahead for certain families. But, thrilling as it can be to foresee the future, it is actually a curse if you can't do anything to change it.

By the time these families of hospice patients were in crisis, I was deeply frustrated to find it was often too late to do much. I wondered what could be done to preempt some of these problems before they reached a critical stage. I vowed to find some kind of preventive medicine for families. I sought ordination as an Episcopal priest and began to study family systems at the postgraduate program of the Bowen Center for the Study of the Family (formerly part of Georgetown Medical School).

As a minister, I found that people confessed to me some things they would not tell their doctors or therapists. Clergy often have access to a family's most private moments, from the joy of weddings and baptisms to the agony of a divorce, kids out of control, or the death of a loved one. The *New York Times* reports that over 40 percent of Americans seek counseling from their clergy, while only 21 percent go to social workers, psychologists, or psychiatrists.[1] It's from these candid revelations that I've been able to piece together the patterns that make a marriage go bad or lead a child to have problems. I also learned what we can do to help preempt their occurrence in our families.

## Learning from Other People's Mistakes

Every story you will read in this book comes from a real family, although I've changed the names and details to protect their privacy. This is a collection of my best insights from almost fifteen years of observing families around the world and hearing real-life confessions of what parents wish they had known before their families descended into crisis. This book centers on three questions:

1. What causes a good marriage to go bad?
2. What causes a child to develop problems?
3. What can you do to prevent these developments in your family, before it's too late?

This book is preventive medicine that can help couples stay happily married and raise happier kids at the same time. If your marriage or your kids are already in trouble, this book will help you understand how you got there and help you to dig yourself out. Unfortunately, to get to the good news, I have to begin with some bad news, which may be a bitter pill for you to swallow. All my time observing families abroad and listening to families at home has convinced me of one thing: Your children's problems are much more connected to your *marriage* than you probably realize.

Our marriages affect our kids in many ways we've barely begun to acknowledge as a society. I know this is terrible news for those of you who try to shield your children from any marital problems you are facing. But we can't deny that kids pick up on everything.

Perhaps you don't want to believe there's any link between your marriage and your children's problems. I acknowledge that my news seems disheartening at first, but ultimately this book offers a liberation you never thought possible, if you can move beyond the initial shock.

Our marriages are in bigger trouble than we think. The press has reported that the divorce rate has leveled off, but that's a misleading statistic. The media usually reports divorce rates on a *per year* basis, but, as marriage expert John Gottman notes, what really matters is the *odds* a marriage that begins in such-and-such a year will eventually end in divorce. And that rate continues to climb rapidly. For example, a couple married in 1890 had only a 10 percent chance of divorce. In 1950 it had risen to 30 percent, and couples married in 1970 had about a 50 percent chance of splitting up. But a couple who got married in 1990 has an estimated 67 percent likelihood of getting a divorce. That means a more recently married couple probably has less than a 30 percent chance of staying married.[2]

Less than 30 percent.

## Couples Living in Emotional Divorce

Many of us like to kid ourselves that we have a good marriage and would never divorce, but a legal divorce should not be our only concern; there are many subtle ways we commit *emotional* divorce from our spouses every day. We avoid touchy topics that make one or both spouses uncomfortable. We avoid making important decisions because we know that discussing them is likely to end in an argument. We avoid sharing our thoughts, feelings, or dreams with our spouse, because it may make us vulnerable to attack or ridicule. Eventually, many couples may end up more like roommates than lovers.

The trouble is that as we move away from our spouse in an emotional divorce, we never remain alone for very long. *We always move toward something or someone else.*

Moving toward something else may mean watching too much TV, becoming obsessed with work, or developing an addiction.

Moving toward someone else does not always mean an extramarital affair. Many emotionally lonely parents find themselves becoming too emotionally attached to their children, often to the children's detriment.

This is not to say emotional attachment to one's child is unhealthy — quite the contrary. The key is to recognize the difference between a healthy attachment to one's child and an unhealthy "marriage" to one's child. When parents seek to meet their own relationship needs through their child, the child ends up bearing an emotional load that the child is not suited to carry. All this parental attention seems child-friendly, but anxious overparenting can lead to serious developmental issues for a child.

Understanding our tendency to marry our children offers freedom from passing our baggage on to our kids. In the first part of this book, I'll help you understand this tendency as clearly and simply as possible. At times it may be a painful journey, but I'll do my best to support you while you take this preventive medicine.

Please take comfort in knowing that you will never be alone on this voyage, because almost every family — including my wife of twelve years and our two children — encounters these same problems in some form or another every day.

In the second part of this book, I offer insight into why we do some of the crazy things we do in families. If your family is like the families I coach, you'll be relieved to find out how we create drama in our families without realizing it. By recognizing our patterns, we can seek to put an end to some of the drama before it begins. I'll offer practical advice that has worked wonders for other families.

## Taking Stock of Your Family

Here are some questions to help you take stock of your family:

• If your child has a problem at school or on the playground, is your first impulse to intervene?

• Do you find it difficult to see your kid struggling or upset?

• Do you strive to be best friends with your child?

If you answered "yes" to any of these questions, you may have bought into a very popular misconception.

## Myth #1: The More Attention We Give Our Kids, The Better They'll Turn Out

Many parents believe the more attention we give our kids, the better they'll turn out, but our kids are not healthier or happier than they were a generation ago. In fact, today's children are more troubled because we've started marrying our kids instead of our spouses.

We claim we're too busy to spend time with our spouses, but actually many of us have shifted our passion from our spouses to our children. We may be overfocusing on our kids to escape an unfulfilling marriage. But if we find it easier to be with our kids than with our spouse, our kids pay a heavy price for that.

As spouses grow more distant in their marriage, they project their distress and needs onto their children. On the surface, things may appear calm between the parents, but kids pick up on everything. Children may soak up the tension in their households until their fragile nervous systems hit overload, and then they act out or develop health problems as a result. Many of today's children are essentially bearing the burden of misplaced stress from their parents' distant marriages. Medical research has already confirmed the link between anxious parents and children with emotional or health problems.

A problem in your child may be a wake-up call for your marriage. Once we become aware of how we are (unknowingly) sabotaging our children's well-being, however, we can step off our current path to harm. Chapters 1 and 2 explain how we mess up our kids with a pattern called "Projection onto Our Children," where our anxious overreaction to a child's problem creates a self-fulfilling prophecy.

This information is crucial because what you don't know *will* hurt you — and your kids. The modern approach to parenting may be turning them into unhappy future adults. Many of today's parents, with the best of intentions, are on a lose–lose path: losing their own marital happiness and losing their child's long-term happiness. The family is the basic building block of society, so until we wake up to this silent crisis in our families, no amount of money or educational reform will fix what ails our families or our nation.

We must regain a balance between tending our marriage and nurturing our children. When our marriages meet our intimacy needs, then we can stop marrying our children. This frees up our kids to establish their own identity, learn self-reliance, and become more independent adults. Our marriage can also set a great example for their future relationships. It's win–win for every member of the family.

## How You Relate to Your Spouse

Here are some questions regarding how you relate to your spouse:

+ When you and your spouse disagree, do you avoid expressing your feelings and talking things out, preferring rather to "keep the peace"?

+ Do you worry after an argument that perhaps you're on your way to divorce?

+ Do you sometimes find it easier to spend time with your kids than with your spouse?

If you answered "yes" to any of these questions, your marriage may be in trouble, even if it seems peaceful. As John Gottman reminds us, even the best marriages still have chronic, unresolved arguments. Arguing is unpleasant, of course, but emotional engagement is better than avoidance.

## Myth #2: Arguing Leads to Divorce

Many couples believe their marriage is strong because they seldom argue. But the *real* silent killer of marriage is when we distance from our spouse in order to keep the peace. We have become experts at justifying how busy we are; most couples have come to believe they simply do not have time for each other. The sad reality is that suddenly, years later, we wake up next to our mate and realize that somewhere along the way, the flame died.

Chapters 3 and 4 explain how we damage our marriages with two patterns: Blaming Our Spouse, and Distancing from Our Spouse. This information is crucial to your family, because blaming your spouse and avoiding him or her may lead you to focus on your child in unhealthy ways.

We will discover the origins of these patterns in our marriages. We can now learn to reduce both our *fight response* of arguing and our *flight response* of avoiding our spouse. Modern neuroscience has confirmed that our fight-or-flight response governs much more of our daily behavior than we realize. It's triggered by an ancient survival instinct we call anxiety.

In our cave man era, anxiety saved our lives by helping us anticipate a threat, but today it causes us to overreact in relationships. By taming the cave man within, we can train our brains to lower that anxiety and become less extreme: less overreactive in our relationships.

## How You View Your Marriage

Next, let's find out how you view your marriage:

+ Do you feel unfulfilled in your marriage?

+ Do you worry that maybe you married the wrong person?

+ Do you feel as though you have matured beyond your spouse, whereas your spouse seems stuck?

Many spouses today secretly wonder if they feel unfulfilled because they married the wrong person. There is no evidence, however, that you'd do better by starting over with someone else. The divorce rate for second marriages is 60 percent, and 73 percent for third marriages.[3]

## Myth #3: If We Feel Unfulfilled in Our Marriage, It's Because We Married the Wrong Person

Chapter 5 explains how our inner anxiety is at the root of the drama in our relationships. This information is crucial because anxiety is what makes us irritable and quick to overreact, and that's what causes drama in families. Once we understand how anxiety works within ourselves, we can notice and manage it to transform our knee-jerk reactions into thoughtful responses.

When we fall in love, that primal *chemistry* we feel is actually Mother Nature's way of scoping out our ideal mate. We're kidding ourselves that the "grass is greener" in a new relationship because we would still carry the same emotional baggage into our next marriage. Marriage is a school for lovers, and the lessons we must learn would be the same the second time around. So, with the exception of spousal abuse, there's no advantage in switching study partners.

Currently, we don't realize our families are caught in a vicious circle of anxiety, blame, distancing, and projection — which in turn lead to *more* anxiety. Chapters 1–5 are designed to open our eyes to the severity and urgency of the problem. Happily, chapters 6 through 10 will help us step out of this vicious circle and build a different kind of marriage that produces happier kids with less baggage.

In chapter 6, I'll explain how Mother Nature gave us chemistry to ensure we married the perfect mate for us. Once we realize the grass is not greener with someone else, we can settle down to create the best marriage possible.

In chapter 7, we'll go on safari in our family of origin to learn how we were programmed for anxiety as children and how we can reduce it as adults.

In chapter 8, we'll discuss how to fix problems in our children by fixing them in ourselves.

In chapter 9, we'll learn how to build the courage to follow through and do what's best for our families in the long run.

And in chapter 10, we'll learn how to build a passionate friendship with our spouse that can last a lifetime.

## Just One Degree of Change
## Alters the Rest of Your Life

My goal is not to sell you a miracle cure, but to help change the course of your family life by only one degree. To use an analogy, imagine you are the captain of a sailing ship. You think you have already charted the best course for your journey, but in fact the course you have chosen will take you over many stormy, dangerous seas. This book will help you alter the course of your journey by one degree.

One degree of change may not seem like much, but with time, your new course takes you further and further from that original, stormy route. Perhaps this change will be enough to keep your marriage intact, whereas you might otherwise have ended up divorced, or with a troubled child.

For some families, their decks are awash with anxiety, and they cannot even see the shoals that lie ahead. This book will give you the awareness you need to avoid the stormy seas before you run aground.

The goal is not to be perfect — no family, including my own, can claim to be — but to start wherever you are and make that one degree of progress. Regardless of the current state of your family, you can improve your marriage and raise happier kids. The stakes are too high, so please don't settle for anything less.

# Part 1

# HOW WE HURT OUR KIDS WITHOUT REALIZING IT

# Chapter One

# How We Create a Self-Fulfilling Prophecy in Our Kids

Sabrina and her husband, Rick, were facing some financial challenges. Rick didn't get the bonus they were expecting, and they were falling behind on their mortgage payments. Every time they tried to discuss the issue, however, they escalated into an argument. As a result, they began to distance from each other. Rick spent more time at the office, and Sabrina paid more attention — perhaps even too much attention — to the kids. When the couple was together, they stuck to banal topics and avoided bringing up any touchy issues — especially money. But unresolved tension pervaded the house, and Sabrina started having trouble sleeping.

One night when she was lying awake, she heard her five-year-old son, Ian, cough in his sleep. Sabrina had already been concerned that perhaps he had asthma or allergies, so when she heard him cough, her anxiety really spiked.

Reflecting on it more, she decided this cough must be serious, and some action needed to be taken. Sabrina got up, woke Ian, gave him cough medicine, went back to bed, and fell asleep almost immediately.

The next morning, as usual, things were tense between Sabrina and her husband as he headed out the door to work.

Sabrina was sitting in the kitchen, alone and upset, when her son came downstairs and coughed again. This time, she picked up the phone and made an appointment with the pediatrician.

The pediatrician's examination of Ian was inconclusive: it could be allergies, he said, or perhaps just a virus. He also noted that Ian hadn't awakened from his cough the night before, or even complained about it. But Sabrina wanted to play it safe, so she persuaded the doctor to prescribe allergy medicine for her son. After all, it was spring, and other mothers had told her how they sent their kids to school with inhalers every day, just to be safe. Who knew how bad the dust and pollen counts might get?

## When It Comes to Attention, Less Is More

Sabrina's example is typical of what's happening in many families today across the country. Why do so many of today's children suffer from emotional and health problems? We parents are often causing or exacerbating these problems through *Projection onto Our Children*. We live in denial about our distant marriages and our stressful lives, but all that anxiety can spill over onto our kids, much to their detriment.

Projection onto Our Children is an unconscious defense mechanism, triggered by a well-intentioned but primitive part of the human brain. Our brain is trying to save us from pain by diverting our attention from our unpleasant anxiety (regarding our distant relationship) to a more pleasant and reassuring image (e.g., becoming best friends with our children or putting them first in our lives).

Our brain has good intentions, but projection just keeps us living in denial: we are projecting our anxiety onto our kids in the form of overparenting. When anxiety becomes unbearable in our brains, we may focus on a small problem in our child in order to take our minds off our own anxiety. This blows the child's problem out of proportion and creates a self-fulfilling prophecy of troubled children. Projection may save us from pain, but it does so at the expense of our children's well-being.

We will address three essential points in this chapter:

1. We parents have gone too far: our anxious attention to our kids is doing more harm than good;

2. We need to recognize the four steps by which we project our anxiety onto our children; and

3. Becoming your child's best friend is just as harmful as anxious worry.

This information is crucial to parents because once we recognize our projection, we can refocus on the real source of the problem: anxiety in ourselves and tension in our marriage.

By tracing a child's anxiety back to the mother, some readers may think I'm blaming the mother for creating the problem. The problem of projection, however, stems from the distant marriage contributed to by both mother and father. Both parents always have a role.

What's more, in most cases, both spouses are innocently unaware of this pattern and have the best of intentions, so how can anyone be blamed? There is no malice here: only a lack of awareness.

## Couples Who Live Like Roommates
## Harm Their Kids

In the 1950s, psychiatrist Murray Bowen set up an experiment at the National Institute of Mental Health where he
observed how schizophrenic patients interacted with their
families. For eighteen months or more, several patients lived
with their entire families in a ward where Bowen and his staff
could observe and record their behaviors 24/7.

As Bowen observed and compared the behavior of these
families, a pattern emerged. He described "a striking emotional distance between the parents in all the families. We have
called this the 'emotional divorce.' ... When either parent
becomes more invested in the patient than in the other parent,
the psychotic process [in their child] becomes intensified."[1]

Bowen's research suggested that a couple's marriage has
more of an impact on their child's well-being than we realize.[2]
As two spouses avoid each other in a distant marriage, one
spouse may focus instead on one of their children. Taken to
the extreme, a distant marriage may lead to a child-focus that
contributes to symptoms in the child's body or mind.

For his work, Bowen was named as one of the top ten
most influential psychiatrists in the last twenty-five years,[3]
and his insights are borne out every day among counselors,
ministers, and researchers. I will never forget the words of
a doctor from Columbia Medical School who specializes in
children's cancer. She said, "I seldom worry about a child's
prognosis when I see her parents fighting with each other.
Cancer is a crisis, and all that stress has to go somewhere. It's
the kid whose parents are distant and reserved that I worry
about."

In the name of love, we intervene too often in our child's welfare. Our children are precious gifts, and of course we would do nothing to harm them — *except* hamper their ability to stand on their own two feet. Psychiatrist Carl Jung believed that the greatest detriment to children was the unlived life of their parents. When the tension goes up in our marriages, we may subconsciously escape by focusing on someone else around us, often our kids. The *New York Times* family columnist and author Judith Warner writes:

> Studies have never shown that total immersion in motherhood makes mothers happy or does their children any good. On the contrary, studies have shown that mothers who are able to make a life for themselves tend to be happy and to make their children happy. The self-fulfillment they get from a well-rounded life actually makes them more emotionally available for their children — in part because they're less needy. . . . [However,] we manage not to acknowledge, despite endless clues from our children's doctors and teachers, that our preferred parenting style is not terribly conducive to promoting future happiness. We persist in doing things that are contrary to our best interests — and our children's best interests. And we continue, against all logic, to subscribe to a way of thinking about motherhood that leaves us guilt-ridden, anxious, and exhausted.[4]

It's time for us to question the status quo, because the status quo is not working. Many of us have come to take for granted that total immersion parenting raises happier kids. And yet, as we look around at our family and friends, where is the evidence? How can all the anxiety, guilt, and fatigue caused by today's parenting style yield happier kids if the parents are increasingly isolated and unhappy themselves? We need to face the fact that the emperor has no clothes — today's children and their parents are suffering more, not less, despite all our frenetic investment of time and attention. In the next section, we will begin to examine how we've created a monster — a parenting monster that is gnawing away at our families' well-being.

## How We Pass On Our Baggage

It was a snowy winter day when I blew into Dr. David Sherry's office to interview him, but I warmed up quickly when he started to tell me about his practice. Dr. Sherry is a pediatric rheumatologist at the nation's top-ranked Children's Hospital of Philadelphia and a professor at the University of Pennsylvania's Medical School. I had heard about his work with over fourteen hundred cases of children who suffer from *amplified musculoskeletal pain:* excruciating pain in their bodies. By the time kids come to him, they have usually undergone multiple tests that have not identified any obvious source of the pain, and multiple medications have failed to provide any relief.

Dr. Sherry has noticed a common pattern in the parents he has met with. They tend to suffer from anxiety, and they make great efforts on behalf of their kids, even to the point of exhaustion. It's as if these parents are hypochondriacs, but instead of imagining themselves to be sick, they (unconsciously) make their child sick, in a kind of self-fulfilling prophecy.

Given the family psychodynamics, a minor pain complaint can increase in severity and dysfunction until these children cannot attend school or go out with friends. Many also develop other symptoms such as headaches, stomachaches, insomnia, dizziness, and breathing difficulties.

"The kids eventually start believing it, too," Sherry says, "and then the parents go from doctor to doctor, bringing with them reams of medical files and test results. These parents keep shopping doctors until they find a physician willing to confirm their amateur diagnosis."

Dr. Sherry jokingly refers to his treatment as a "parentectomy." He stops all medications, limits parental contact, and conducts a psychological evaluation. The children also undergo six hours of exercise each day for three weeks, which not only increases blood flow to their muscles, but also helps them sleep better.

His cure rate is over 88 percent, and the cure lasts at least five years, according to his follow-up evaluations.

Despite his success, Dr. Sherry is concerned about how widespread the problem is. Lately, he sees more kids who are anorexic, depressed, or suicidal. They may even act out with drugs, behavior disorders, or promiscuous sex. He sometimes feels as though he's just putting Band-Aids on an epidemic of symptoms, rather than addressing the family dynamics that cause these problems. He remarks, "I see many children suffer due to the stress of covert marital discord. When spouses distance from each other, they sometimes make their child the center of their lives, which interferes with the natural weaning process essential to healthy development. The best gift you can give your kids is to create a good marriage.

Unfortunately, this is much easier said than done and getting the family to address these underlying issues can be too threatening for them."

As a pediatrician and a minister, Dr. Sherry and I see many troubled children from families in which the parents believe their marriage is good merely because they never raise their voices at one another. But their relations are characterized by distance: the husband may work long hours or travel often, or perhaps he bowls in three different leagues a week. We'll discuss Distancing from Your Spouse in chapter 4, but for now, let's just say it's almost as if the husband has checked out of the marriage.

Either party can be the cause, though, and both partners play some role: perhaps the husband checked out because his wife became too focused on the kids, or perhaps the wife began to "marry" her kids because the husband was emotionally unavailable. In any event, her focus frequently falls on one child in particular. As the author and child psychologist Madeline Levine memorably observes, "When a marriage is cold, a child's bed is a warm place to be."[5]

It may *seem* child-friendly to give a child more attention, but if a caregiver makes the child the center of her life, it puts too much pressure on the kid. The two may become best friends rather than parent-child, making it difficult to set the boundaries by which a child learns to work on teams or respect the authority of her teachers. If a parent leans too much on a child to meet her intimacy needs, this creates a co-dependence between parent and child that hampers the child's social skills with her peers.[6]

On a subconscious level, our brain has the best of intentions when it diverts our attention from the painful reality of our anxiety to an overfocus on our child. But this projection inadvertently prolongs and intensifies our problems by keeping us in denial. Instead of addressing the problems in our marriage or in ourselves that led to our high anxiety, we ignore our pain. On some level, we convince ourselves that pouring our attention onto our child is loving, unselfish, and altruistic. But the child soaks up our anxiety until her fragile nervous system hits overload, and then she may develop a symptom.[7]

## The Four Steps of Projection onto Our Children

How do a parent's intangible feelings of anxiety become tangible, physical symptoms in her child? Returning to our earlier story, Sabrina's worry about Ian's cough in the night is an example of how too much negative, worried attention can create a self-fulfilling prophecy in a child.

Shifting our attention from our spouse to a child can make the child into a scapegoat for our own distant marriage. If Sabrina and her husband were more aware of the level of tension between them, they might handle it better. But all that anxiety and intensity in their relationship requires some kind of outlet, so they unwittingly spray some of that anxiety onto their child, and that's when the child develops behavior problems or an ailment.

Think of this spraying of anxiety onto the child in terms of the mind-body connection. Until recently, perhaps we envisioned the mind-body connection as simply *our* minds influencing *our own* bodies. For example, maybe we would be more likely to catch a cold when we're stressed because stress lowers our immune response. Many of us who work with families have suspected, however, that this is just the tip of the iceberg, and researchers such as John Cacioppo are beginning to quantify a larger mind-body connection.

Cacioppo is a University of Chicago psychologist who conducted a large study of the impact of relationships on health. He concludes that our minds (unknowingly) affect not only our own bodies but the bodies of our loved ones as well — even on a daily basis. The feelings we subtly communicate, beneath our awareness, are soaked up by our loved ones and affect their own feelings, which in turn affects their own health. And "the more significant the relationship is in your life, the more it matters for your health."[8] In other words, if you're anxious, it may lower your own immune response and make you vulnerable to colds. But anxiety is contagious, so your feelings may be lowering the immune response of your loved ones as well.

In an anxious family such as Sabrina's, where the caregiver is overfocused on her child, this emotional enmeshment between parent and child may program the child to internalize the stress of others and manifest it in health or social problems. It's as if this child becomes the "identified patient" who bears the symptoms of the family's unrest.

Dr. Michael Kerr, a psychiatrist at the Bowen Center for the Study of the Family, studies this kind of projection in families. He stresses that in the pattern of Projection onto Our Children, no one is to blame because every step of this pattern takes place beneath the awareness of the parent and child. The parents don't realize how anxious they are and how they spray their anxiety onto the child by overreacting to a perceived problem in the kid.

When the child finally manifests a symptom, the parents don't realize they're dodging the tension in their marriage by focusing on the child and anxiously seeking a diagnosis. Once a doctor pronounces a diagnosis for the alleged problem, or prescribes a medication, what started out as a small problem suddenly gets blown out of proportion, creating a self-fulfilling prophecy that can cripple the child's development.[9]

The steps in the process of Projection onto Our Children are not that complicated once you learn about them, but they may be shocking or overwhelming to read for the first time. Perhaps we've never looked at how we parent from this perspective before. Perhaps we can recognize ourselves in these steps — and that could feel quite uncomfortable.

We parents already have a lot of guilt, and we feel pressure to "get it right." My goal is not to add more guilt. Rather, I'm trying to provide a way of looking at the problem that could be liberating, because if we can get to the root of the cause, we can begin to fix it. We need to address the cause, rather than getting caught up in all the symptoms.

At first, it's painful to see how we might have been hurting a loved one without realizing it. But it's short-term pain for long-term gain. There's no need to beat ourselves up; we didn't know we were doing it until now. And the long-term gain is that we can nip our projection in the bud before it has any more ill effects on our children. That's good news for you and your family. Our families are truly worth the struggle; they are, after all, where much of our happiness in this world resides.

Let's walk through the steps of Projection onto Our Children, this time breaking down the steps of the pattern in more detail.

### Step 1: The Parent's Anxiety Seeks an Outlet

Suppose a mother is anxious. Why is this process centered on the mother? Like it or not, the mother tends to be the primary caregiver in most families. In all of our ape cousins, the mother is the primary caregiver. This mother-infant bond is generally acknowledged in humans as well. This tendency may shift, however, as more fathers take on primary caregiver roles.

In a later chapter we'll discuss in detail how anxiety can trigger the fight-or-flight response with one's spouse. For now, let's just say that the mother and father either argue a lot or they play "let's pretend things are fine by avoiding all touchy topics" — both of which may escalate the anxiety already present in the marriage.

As the distance or arguing increase in her marriage, the caregiver's demons get the best of her, and her self-doubts may begin to feel overwhelming. These days, few families enjoy the benefit of an extended family or a supportive informal community of women, so many caregivers feel increased loneliness and insecurity about how to parent. For example, back in the days when a caregiver might live near her mother and even grandmother, they constantly communicated, "*This* is the correct way to parent." It didn't matter so much if their advice was right or wrong. What mattered was that they communicated certainty, and this inspired confidence in the caregiver as she faced the daily onslaught of self-doubt in her parenting decisions.

But today, parents often parent in isolation. We lack the reassuring wisdom and mentoring of the older generations. Instead, we face the disparate, demanding voices of experts who communicate via schools and the media.

Thus, it's hardly surprising that a caregiver's unsureness and fear of "doing it wrong" often get the best of her, and she may feel overwhelmed by feelings of inadequacy. These worried feelings may permeate her thinking and cause her brain to "overheat" with anxiety, such that it triggers a safety valve to relieve the pressure and allow the excess anxiety to escape.

This safety valve is an unconscious process called scapegoating or projection. Typically, the caregiver first feels overwhelmed; then her anxiety eventually becomes too uncomfortable to bear. So her brain tries to protect her by switching on the safety valve, an instinctive defense mechanism that diverts her attention away from her unpleasant feelings. The problem is that a caregiver has no control over *where* that excess anxiety sprays.

Kerr observes how a caregiver begins to offload her anxiety onto her child through projection: "The dominant one projects or 'sprays' [her] anxiety and, in the process, usually feels calmer; the adaptive one [i.e., the child] picks up or absorbs the anxiety and, in the process, becomes more anxious and more at risk for a symptom."[10]

In other words, suddenly a caregiver notices a small defect, real or perceived, in her child's health, social skills, or learning ability. This is the problem she will project her anxiety onto until it becomes amplified. Humans rarely scapegoat anyone on purpose, and certainly not a beloved child. But when our mind is overwhelmed with anxiety and our brain triggers the safety valve to protect us from pain, we have little conscious control over where that excess anxiety is directed. Those closest to us usually bear the brunt, especially sensitive kids, who pick up on everything. This primitive defense mechanism is clumsy and unfair, but it is truly a force to be reckoned with.

Kerr describes how "an escalating cycle of anxiety and problem behavior would then ensue and result in the 'anxious one' getting into more of a caretaking position than he or she wanted, and the 'problem one' getting into more of a patient or child position than he or she wanted."[11]

### Step 2: The Caregiver Seeks Affirmation from Experts

Doctors privately lament the number of anxious parents who bring in kids with psychosomatic symptoms created by both the parent and the child playing off each other. In the old days, parents ascribed more authority to doctors, and doctors took more time with their patients. So a doctor might have been able to calm a caregiver's fears by saying, "I see many of these cases each month, and I think you've let your worry get the best of you. Your son will be just fine, and it's all in your head."

I believe doctors are as compassionate today as they've ever been, but they are under tremendous pressure. In today's world, doctors are more highly specialized and more pushed for time, and parents no longer view them as infallible. For many doctors it may be easier to write a prescription than persuade some parents that their worried focus actually contributes to their child's poor health.

Doctors I've interviewed say they would rather keep their office visits short than play psychologist and risk a confrontation. They feel it's pointless to try to convince these caregivers their child may not have an ailment at all, and doctors don't get paid any extra for a ten-minute, gut-churning argument. Besides, the parent will probably just go get her diagnosis from another doctor anyway and the doctor will lose a client or, worse yet, if by chance there *is* some ailment the doctor missed, then the doctor may have a lawsuit on her hands.

So the doctors don't intend any harm, but in their rush to see patients and keep the peace, they may end up enabling this projection process. Once the caregiver finds an expert to confirm that her molehill is indeed a mountain, the caregiver acts as though her diagnosis is self-evident.

### Step 3: The Family Jumps on Board

By this point, other family members may have bought into the family projection process as well, and everyone begins to treat the child differently. They make special allowances. They infantilize or overprotect the child and may spend many hours on research, treatments, appointments, or medication for the "problem" their child has.

### Step 4: Now the Child Also Buys into the Projection Process

The final step in this process is when even the child buys into the projection process. On some level, he may be thinking, "Mommy knows best. I must have a problem." And even if he has any doubts, he's powerless to resist her, unable to articulate his objections.

So he unconsciously sacrifices some of his own well-being in order to ensure a calm, stable relationship with his caregiver. If his caregiver is anxious, a child becomes anxious by osmosis. Thus, it's in his best interest to calm his caregiver in any way he can and reduce her anxiety level. Absorbing some of his caregiver's excess anxiety and developing a symptom seems like a small price to pay to have a calm caregiver. If he complies with her assessment, it ensures that the care on which he depends will continue, or perhaps even increase.[12]

Of course, Projection onto Our Children does not explain every child's ailment. Sometimes there are real physical symptoms, but the family projection process can exacerbate even genuine symptoms that are not psychosomatic. It's like throwing gasoline on a small fire: the child's symptom was small until the parent sprayed the gasoline of her anxiety all over it.

It's extremely difficult for us as parents to explore how we may be projecting onto our kids. Instead, we may prefer to focus on other causes of our children's problems. One of the most popular explanations for today's troubled children is genetics.

## Nature versus Nurture

Many parents want to believe our children's ailments are genetic, because we would feel guilty to discover we play a role in our child's suffering. The truth is that we do and will play a part in our children's struggles — how could we not? Further, medical research has confirmed several of the ways in which we harm our child's well-being without even realizing it. We owe it to our children to set aside our guilt and denial, in order to learn how we may be causing them — and our marriages — real damage.

Sure, it's bad news to find out we may be harming our kids, but beating ourselves up is counterproductive. Instead, let's rejoice in the great news that we have more control over our kids' well-being than we might have thought. There are three points that can empower you to enhance your family's well-being:

1. When it comes to our children's health problems, genetics are not the simple, guilt-free explanation we had expected. We cannot explain away our children's problems as bad luck or fate.

2. A child's family environment plays a considerable role in creating children's ailments. This news may sting at first, but our kids will benefit in the long run.

3. Our minds have much more impact on our loved-ones' bodies than we realize. Medical research confirms that anxiety in the mind of a parent can cause emotional or physical symptoms in the body of a child.

Many people believe that today's common child ailments, such as learning disabilities, ADHD, allergies, asthma, autism, and obesity are mostly genetic. Since the human genome was decoded in 2003, top genetic scientists have been searching for the gene that causes a particular disease. Over one hundred studies in several countries, conducted on thousands of patients, have found some genes, or combinations of genes, that are indeed linked to a given disease. "But in almost all cases they carry only a modest risk for the disease. Most of the genetic link to disease remains unexplained," according to Harvard and Duke geneticists quoted in the *New York Times*.[13]

In other words, some children with a genetic predisposition to a certain ailment may develop severe symptoms, but other kids with the same predisposition develop mild symp-toms or none at all.[14] There is significant research reminding us not to blame genetics for our children's problems.[15]

There is, however, another solution to the genetic mystery: family environment plays a considerable role in children's ail-ments.[16] In many cases, children do indeed "inherit" ailments from their parents, but *not genetically*. Parents pass on their baggage through the mind-body connection, and it begins even as early as the womb. Here's how:

Many readers are familiar with how a mother's eating habits affect the developing child in the womb, as nutrients pass through her placenta. Likewise, a mother "programs" her infant's immune system in the womb by passing valu-able antibodies in her bloodstream through her placenta to the fetus — a priceless legacy of disease-fighting know-how. These are examples of a well-documented phenomenon called "Prenatal Programming."[17]

Unfortunately, there are also negative examples of Prenatal Programming. A mother who smokes or drinks too much, for example, can negatively impact her child's health. So it is also that a mother can pass on her anxiety through the placenta. While a child is *in utero,* an anxious mother's stress hormones, such as cortisol, pass through her placenta into her amniotic fluid. As her baby grows inside her, the fetal brain and body develop within what is literally a "bath of anxiety," which may program the fetus to overreact to stress. The presence of too much cortisol affects the developing tissues and neurons, making them overly sensitive: they react too early, and too strongly, to stimuli.

This may predispose a child to the emotional oversensitivity found in autism and depression, or the oversensitivity of body tissues associated with food or skin allergies, or the inflamed bronchial passages of asthma.[18]

In other words, in many cases, a child doesn't inherit a gene from her parents that causes an ailment in her body. It may be the tension in the parents' marriage, which causes anxiety in the pregnant mother and alters the development of the tissue and neurons in the fetus. One could say the fetus "inherits" illnesses from the anxious environment of her family. As parents, our minds have much more impact on our children's bodies than we realize.

Once a child is born with a given sensitivity, anxious parents continue to pass on their anxiety through overparenting. Their worry and obsessive monitoring of the child may magnify her problem. The famous pediatrician T. Berry Brazelton observes that overparenting is a phenomenon well-known to pediatricians. Medical research refers to it as "Vulnerable Child Syndrome." Caregivers who feel anxious or insecure begin to overprotect their child, which programs her for learned helplessness.[19]

Perhaps it's a combination of Vulnerable Child Syndrome and Prenatal Programming that explains today's epidemic of troubled children and overparenting. Maybe a fetus has already been programmed to have defects by the time it is born, and an anxious parent with a distant marriage may be predisposed to transforming any problem from a minor concern into a major one.

Some people point to environmental factors unrelated to family dynamics (such as pollution or mercury in vaccinations). But family environment still matters. One may debate how much projection contributes to children's mental and physical ailments, but compelling research has shown that the anxiety that leads to projection is indeed a factor.[20] In my experience with families, it appears to be a very large factor.

## The Mind-Body Connection: Our Minds Affect Our Kids' Bodies

Below are three examples of ailments that appear genetic, but may actually involve Prenatal Programming and Vulnerable Child Syndrome:

Many parents believe that autism is genetically inherited.[21] However, Dr. Paul Law, who works at a top-flight research center known as the Kennedy Krieger Institute in Baltimore, has developed some compelling statistics. Dr. Law administers a database comprised of over ten thousand families with at least one autistic child. The database is called the Interactive Autism Network. Dr. Law reports his data show that over half of the mothers were themselves diagnosed with depression before they ever had an autistic child.[22]

One may debate whether anxiety causes depression or depression causes anxiety, but the two tend to appear together. So the common denominator in these mothers of autistic children may be an unusually high level of anxiety and depression, and doctors have identified marital problems as the single largest cause of depression.[23] In other words, a distant marriage may contribute to anxious, depressed mothers, and too many stress hormones in the mother's amniotic fluid may alter the brain tissues of the fetus and contribute to autism.

Genetics simply cannot explain why over 50 percent of families with an autistic child have mothers who were diagnosed as depressed even before the birth of that child. Even if we imagine that there's a "depression gene" that is somehow linked to the "autism gene," depression and autism are increasing much more rapidly than these genes could spread. Even if autism and depression *are* genetic, it would take generations for enough of these bad genes to spread through our population. There is probably something more at play than DNA or better standards of diagnosis.

A second example of the mind-body connection and Projection onto Our Children is food allergies. In 2001, Susan Dominus reported in the *New York Times Magazine* how some anxious parents blow symptoms in their children out of proportion, thus contributing to a diagnosis of allergies that may not be accurate. Dominus quotes Dr. Hugh Sampson, chief of the division of pediatric allergy and immunology at Mount Sinai Medical Center: "Hypochondria is a big problem in this area.... There's definitely a certain personality type." Sampson describes certain parents who seem to have a strange fixation on their children's alleged food allergies, treating these allergies as self-evident even in the absence of evidence.[24]

ADHD (attention deficit hyperactivity disorder) is a third example of how the mind-body connection can manifest as Prenatal Programming, Vulnerable Child Syndrome, or both. For example, perhaps an anxious mother's stress hormones affected the impulse-control centers of her fetus's brain, so the child was born with hyperactivity. Or perhaps an anxious parent overreacts to her child's impulsive behavior and creates a self-fulfilling prophecy that ends up diagnosed as ADHD. Either way, prominent neuroscientist Jaak Panksepp believes we parents now overreact to what used to be a normal activity: rough-and-tumble play.

Rough-and-tumble play used to fall within the range of normal behavior, but somewhere along the line, it became pathologized as a neurological illness with a diagnosis of attention deficit hyperactivity disorder. Dr. Panksepp suggests that the behavior of children didn't change so much as parents' and teachers' unwillingness to tolerate it. In the past, kids who squirmed in their seats and didn't pay attention got all their impulsiveness out on the playground during recess. Today, a dramatic number of kids are often forced to take medications. Dr. Panksepp expresses concern about this trend:

> Are excessively playful children now being medicated to reduce their natural desire to play, on the pretext that they have some type of impulse-control disorder? This seems to be the case for at least some of the children who are being medicated. If so, it is unconscionable to give them antiplay drugs such as methylphenidate instead of providing substantial opportunities for rough-and-tumble play at the appropriate times of day, such as early in the morning when such urges are especially high. Even more frightening is the fact that the nervous system becomes sensitized to psychostimulants, and animal research indicates that such modifications of the nervous system can be permanent. Are we now permanently altering the nervous systems of children with psychostimulant medications? Might we not actually be retarding the natural growth of the brain by reducing the normal influence of playful behaviors on central nervous system development?[25]

Disciplining an unruly child is one thing, but giving him medication to squelch what used to be normal behavior is another. These medications for ADHD have become routine treatment, but Panksepp draws a distinction between what's common and what's normal. It may have become common to give a child medication, but there's nothing normal about permanently altering his brain development. And yet, in today's frenzy of parents' Projection onto Our Children, we accept such drastic measures as medication with hardly a shudder anymore. And our children naturally follow their parents' lead.

The above three examples represent only the tip of the iceberg regarding the impact of Prenatal Programming, Vulnerable Child Syndrome, and Projection onto Our Children. The sooner we become aware of the mind-body connection in our parenting, the brighter our children's futures will be.

## Projection Summarized

So let's review the four steps of Projection onto Our Children using the example above of Sabrina's response to Ian's cough. In Step 1, Sabrina is feeling anxious and tense because of their financial challenges, which she and her husband find difficult to discuss without arguing or stomping away. In Step 2, Sabrina overreacts to Ian's harmless cough, assumes he has allergies, and convinces Ian's (skeptical) pediatrician to prescribe allergy medication.

Step 3 includes a significant transition from anxious feelings in one parent to a tangible reality in the family. Sabrina reports the pediatrician's "diagnosis" to her husband as if it were clear-cut. The husband trusts the expert's opinion, especially since it seems plausible in the face of all the buzz about allergies he hears from friends, neighbors, and the media.

Both parents now believe strongly enough in the diagnosis to act, so they "allergy-proof" the house on Ian's behalf, and they carry his allergy meds with them whenever they go out, "just in case."

Finally in Step 4, Ian is persuaded by the certainty exhibited in his parents' behavior toward him, and soon he takes it for granted that he must have allergies. He reduces his outdoor exercise and activities, which makes him less healthy in the long run.

Notice that the parents never address their inability to work through their marital tension because they have focused exclusively on Ian's alleged ailment. Unfortunately, once this pattern of projection has been established, it's likely to occur again the next time there's tension between the parents.

This negative attention to a child's small problem is the most common form of Projection onto Our Children, but there's also another type, which is even harder to spot because it seems desirable. It is too much positive attention lavished on a child, and I refer to it as the Best Friends Syndrome.

## Your Child Is Not Your Best Friend

Christine was diagnosed with mild depression just after she married. In therapy she concluded it was because she didn't receive enough love as a child. Christine vowed she would be different from her parents, so when her daughter, Allison, was born, Christine was a beacon of positive reinforcement and attention. All of Allison's childhood drawings were received with glowing praise, as if they were works of art. Christine smiled at Allison's tantrums, laughing them off as "feisty," even though the behavior had grown so intolerable that Christine's friends now hesitated to invite them over for dinner. It was as if Allison could do no wrong, and nothing was too good for her in Christine's eyes.

As Allison entered adolescence, she didn't seem to have much of a rebellious phase. She and her mother remained close, and Christine would brag to neighbors, "Allison is my best friend. She'll even *tell* you we're best friends." They would finish each other's sentences, and seemed almost inseparable. Even when Allison went off to college, they would call or text each other over a dozen times a day....

Modern society tells us to put our kids first. Almost everyone in your family, your school, and the media believes that the more attention you give your kids, the better they'll turn out. The experts seem to agree that parents should minimize any trauma that might scar a child, perhaps for life. According to one recent report, today's married fathers spend twice as much time with their kids as they did in 1965, and mothers spend 20 percent more time.[26]

What's happening to these parent-child relationships as kids grow up and move on to college? One study of fifteen universities estimated that 40 to 60 percent of college parents now fit the category of helicopter parents, hovering over their children to ensure they always feel supported and get the best treatment possible.[27]

Yet, with all this increased attention to our kids, where are the results? Today there are more troubled kids and more single parents than ever before. Anyone who has taught school for longer than ten years can tell you that the number of students taking drugs for health problems, antisocial behavior, and learning disabilities has skyrocketed. For decades we've been killing ourselves to give our kids every opportunity in life, but they seem more troubled, they sometimes "fail to launch," and we're left anxious and exhausted.

Child specialist Dr. Benjamin Spock had already predicted over forty years ago where we'd end up. In a 1960 article, "Russian Children Don't Whine, Squabble or Break Things — Why?" he worried that one of the fathers of psychology, Sigmund Freud, was being misinterpreted. We thought Freud meant we should avoid causing any anger or sadness in our children, because it scars them. But Freud never meant we shouldn't enforce clear rules of acceptable behavior. He never meant that we should condone inappropriate behavior as a child's "essential self-expression."[28]

Overparenting can be just as anxious (and just as harmful) if it's too positive rather than too negative. The most common example of anxious, overpositive parenting is parents who try to create perfect, trauma-free childhoods for our children. All the guilt and irritation we suppress in order to do so ends up causing more harm than the trauma we had hoped to prevent.

Somewhere along the line, we lost confidence in our own common sense, and now our uncertainty, anxiety, and guilt have overwhelmed our ability to parent our kids calmly and firmly. Spock was right: we took Freud too far, and now we're in a mess.

In the short term, it seems loving to become best friends with your child, but as we'll examine in detail in the next chapter, it hampers her growth and transition into an independent adult. That's how we inadvertently program our children for unhappiness in the long term. Whatever our good intentions, that's not the kind of love we want to give our children.

Most parents would never dream that making their children the center of their lives could be harmful. They believe they just don't have time for their spouse because they're busy putting their children first. But the truth is parents may feel more love for their kids than they do for their spouse. Parents convince themselves that being best friends is child-friendly, but in doing so they cause at least four problems:

First, it becomes harder to discipline our kids because we always want to be their best friends. This opens the door to a child simply badgering his parents until he gets his way. The child's future boss and spouse, however, may not be as patient with this behavior.

Second, if we make the kids the center of our family, our marriage soon dries up, and we interact less like lovers and more like work colleagues discussing logistics.

Third, giving our kids more attention may make us feel like good parents in the short term, but our gift of attention is tainted by neediness. If we need affection from our kids that we should be getting from our spouses, then we're making our kids pay for our inability to face our marriage. If our marriage is difficult and we turn to our kids for intimacy, it puts unhealthy pressure on them to fulfill our emotional needs, which may lead to the children becoming the "identified patient," the symptom-bearer of the family's unrest.[29]

Fourth, being best friends with our child contributes to their failure to launch when they reach their twenties, because they suffer from arrested development. These kids can't take care of themselves, they don't want to take care of themselves, and consequently we come to believe we have no choice but to take care of them.

To summarize, too much attention — whether it's worried attention or affectionate attention — can create an identified patient in the family. But most overparenting combines an anxious focus on perceived defects with a best-friends approach, giving our children the worst of both worlds.

## A Wake-Up Call

If you find yourself wringing your hands about some aspect of your child's behavior, let that be a wake-up call for your marriage. Instead of trying to create perfect childhoods for your kids by making them the center of your universe, you should focus on creating a good marriage.

Studies have shown that the best way to make children happy is for their caregivers to create fulfilled lives for themselves. A fulfilled parent is less needy. It's not about how much time we spend with our children, or making them the center of our lives. (That just leaves parents anxious and exhausted.) What matters is our ability to limit the guilt and neediness we bring into the relationship with our children.[30]

We don't realize the love we give our kids may be tainted by neediness, which hampers the natural weaning process. Weaning is an instinctive process we humans share with all mammals, but if our anxiety and neediness take over our instincts to let our children grow to healthy independence, our children pay a huge price for that. We'll take a look at weaning in chapter 2.

# Chapter Two

# Why We Kill Our Kids with Kindness

## How versus Why

In chapter 1, we examined Projection onto Our Children and how too much attention actually harms our kids instead of helping them. In this chapter, we'll discuss *why* that is the case. Consider this story:

Ann had her share of insecurities, and she believed they stemmed from not receiving enough love from her mother. Thus, when Ann became a mother herself, she was determined to give her daughter, Nina, all the love and attention she needed. In this way she would ensure that Nina had good self-esteem and would grow up happy.

Ann's strategy seemed to work well in her daughter's first ten years. They got along smoothly, and whenever Nina was upset about something, Ann spent more time with her and showed her more love.

After puberty, however, Nina started acting out at school and her grades plummeted. Ann assumed she needed more attention and positive reinforcement, but no matter how much she reassured her, it didn't seem to help Nina feel better.

As a teen, Nina began to feel that her mother had let her down. From Nina's point of view, ever since she was a little girl, she had worked hard to be a "good kid" for her mom. She was sensitive to her mother's moodiness, and at a young age Nina tacitly began to take responsibility for keeping her mother calm. For example, when her mother came home tired from work, Nina made sure to quickly obey her mother's commands, such as cleaning up her room extra carefully, so as not to upset her. When her mother was irritable because she was having trouble with her boss, Nina played more quietly so as not to disturb her.

On some level, Nina felt she had always been there for her mother when Ann was upset. Perhaps in return, Nina *unconsciously* had high expectations for her mother. So when Nina began to feel troubled and unhappy in her teens, Nina felt let down that her mother couldn't fix things for her. Nina felt strongly that her mother had not kept her end of the loving, giving bargain.

"She ought to know what I need!" was a common refrain in her mind. At the time when all her friends got training bras, Nina was furious that her mother hadn't cared enough to buy one for her — although Nina had never asked. Nina was shocked when she got her first period, and blamed her mother because Ann had never sat down to explain things fully to Nina. At the time, it never occurred to Nina to communicate these feelings with her mother.

So, the bitterness festered inside Nina, and she looked for ways to avoid her mom, who didn't seem to understand Nina the way she had always understood her mother. Nina showed her resentment by shunning her and hanging out with the wrong crowd. Ironically, Nina seemed even more angry toward Ann than Ann had felt toward her own mother.

Ann sensed the bitterness in her daughter, and she redoubled her efforts to show kindness and love toward Nina. But it never seemed to be enough. Ann couldn't understand it: she agreed with society's popular notion that kids develop problems because they feel neglected or unloved. Yet she didn't see how she could have been any more loving toward Nina — it just didn't make sense. . . . [1]

Sure, some children become troubled because they were neglected. But the majority of today's children aren't troubled because they lack attention. They receive too much.

In chapter 1, we began to see how anxious overparenting is what causes many of today's children to have many more problems than we — or our parents — did. In this chapter, we're going to go deeper and explain *why* we feel so tempted to get emotionally wrapped up with our children in unhealthy ways. We're going to uncover the unconscious, unhealthy process by which we may program our children for anxious, unhappy adulthoods.

It all has to do with weaning. Today's parents have forgotten how to wean.

Popular psychology is correct that a child's early interactions with her primary caregivers do indeed shape her personality, but *not at all in the way we think*. It's not about going to extremes of showering our children with attention and positive reinforcement. It's about striking a balance between forging a bond and weaning a child toward emotional independence.

In order to relearn how to wean, parents first need to discover how we pass our anxieties onto our kids through a daily interaction we're not even aware of known as *attunement*. Once we understand attunement, we can begin to treat one cause of problems in our families instead of just treating the symptoms.

We will address eight essential points in this chapter:

1. Just as other animals wean their offspring, we humans must also wean our children toward independence.

2. The mother-infant bond is a temporary attachment of a caregiver to her infant to ensure that the infant thrives.

3. But it's not just a loving mother caring for her naïve baby. Attunement is a constant, complex, and significant *two-way* interaction between them.

4. Weaning is a crucial step to ensure a child grows to emotional independence.

5. If the child's weaning is impaired, caregiver and child may become too attached.

6. When a caregiver is too attached, she and her child both become "addicted" to each other in a kind of co-dependence that stunts the development of both. Everybody loses.

7. This mother-child addiction steps up their overreactions to each other, and their increasing misattunement programs the child to be anxious and act out.

8. When the child grows up, he will replicate this "drama" in his adult relationships.

Understanding attunement and how the weaning process goes awry is crucial, because these are primary ways we pass our baggage on to our kids. This chapter will discuss how we can get stuck in the mother-infant bond, which leads to Incomplete Weaning. This Incomplete Weaning affects our attunement with our child, and we begin unconsciously sending the wrong messages to our child, which programs him for anxiety and acting out. (The other two ways we pass our baggage on to our kids are Projection, as we saw in chapter 1, and Imprinting, as we'll see in chapter 5.)

But first, a note on language in this chapter. Wherever possible, I have used the gender-neutral term "caregiver" to indicate mother or father. Whereas the mother-infant bond is well-documented in research on both primates and humans, the same bond with dads may become apparent as more fathers take on primary caregiver roles.

Right now, if you're like most of us, you probably run ragged each day to provide more time, attention, and support to your child. So take heart: my solution will turn out much easier than the time-and-energy-consuming process you're engaged in now. By the end of this chapter you'll see why your child is far better off if you stop killing yourself and your marriage in order to give him "the perfect childhood."

While a healthy mother-infant bond is critical at certain developmental stages, a healthy weaning process ensures a child reaches independence. In the modern era, we have gone overboard in embracing and prolonging the mother-infant bond, to the detriment of our children's long-term healthy independence. This chapter will help to bring the primal weaning process into our awareness, so we can manage it more thoughtfully.

## Like All Animals,
## Humans Wean Their Offspring

A key to understanding the weaning process is to remember that humans are animals too. Although we have a higher level of self-consciousness than other animals, neuroscience research shows that instincts still play an important role in our primal behaviors, such as mating and raising offspring. The take-away for us is that we can learn a lot from observing our animal cousins.[2]

There are many interesting examples of weaning in nature. You've probably heard the stories about how eagles will push their young fledglings out of their clifftop nests, in order to teach them to fly. That's a rather abrupt transition. Perhaps some people will accept it as nature's way, yet when it comes to pushing a young human out of the nest, these same individuals may have a sharply different reaction.

As a boy growing up on our farm, I would observe cattle with their newborn calves. It was hard to watch, but there came a point when the calf would try to nurse and the mother cow would kick the calf away. This kick was no gentle love tap. I watched the calves go flying, sprawled like Bambi with their forelegs stuck out — and I thought, "That ain't love! What is that? Doesn't the mommy cow love her calf?"

At the time, I didn't make the connections I now see, but I do remember seeing those calves were soon eating grass and foraging on their own. They took care of themselves, because they had to. And likewise with those eagle chicks; they learned how to fly because they had to. There is a standard amount of time for each species before the mother nudges her infant from her breast and no longer gives her offspring constant attention. Mother Nature knows that the survival of offspring depends on their ability to achieve independence within a reasonable period after birth. Mammals leave their parent's side in order to explore, hunt, and eventually find a mate of their own.

Again, the key point to remember is that humans are animals too. We parents also have an instinct to wean, although funny movies like *Failure to Launch* with Matthew McConaughey show how we may have lost touch with that instinct. In order to remind us of our weaning instincts, we need to start with the instinct that precedes weaning, namely, the mother-infant bond.

## The Mother-Infant Bond: Ensuring Her Infant Will Thrive

Our human version of the mother-infant bond strongly resembles that of our primate cousins. With pregnancy, a rush of extra estrogen and progesterone prime the female's maternal instincts. At birth, a cascade of prolactin and oxytocin takes over, motivating primate mothers to nurture, feed, and protect their offspring until they are mature enough to begin to fend for themselves. From rats to monkeys, oxytocin is what lubricates the relationship between caregiver and offspring. In experiments when scientists have blocked the flow of oxytocin, caregivers of many species lose interest in their offspring and no longer make the usual overtures to their babies.[3]

The mother-infant bond in humans is good news, because it guarantees a child's survival. Our child becomes the center of our world, and our parenting hormones help us ignore the sleep deprivation, the stinky diapers, and the colic (ever been there?). For example, if a baby cries, it is thanks to the mother-infant bond that the caregiver can't bear to hear her child's suffering. It's almost as if she has an "empathy overload," in that her child's suffering elicits such discomfort in her that she cannot help but soothe and take care of that child's needs right away. Studies have shown the power of a mother's neurological response to the sound of her own child's cries in particular.[4]

We may nod at this familiar empathy a caregiver feels for her child, but it may not have occurred to us that this empathy is mutual. A baby is also highly tuned to his caregiver's voice and body language. Mother Nature has equipped him with the ability to charm his caregiver, be adorable, and otherwise build rapport in a myriad of delightful ways. But he doesn't do this for fun.

Babies are born much smarter than we realize, because their brains hit the ground running. Some neuroscientists and psychologists have studied the way a baby instinctively knows how to cry, gesture, and communicate his caregiving needs. In fact, the wired-in ability of offspring to elicit the care they need is common to most animal newborns, from birds to monkeys.[5] A baby has been programmed to instinctively pursue his best interests: survival and thriving. He does this by establishing a rapport with his caregiver, and this relationship is his best insurance that maternal care will continue as long as possible.[6]

## Attunement: A Conversation between Caregiver and Child

Scientists refer to this dance of rapport between mother and child as *attunement,* and it's one of the most important concepts you'll read in this book. As the name implies, attunement means caregiver and child are literally "tuned in" to each other and mirror each other's emotions.

There are two key points to remember about attunement:

First, attunement is a highly sensitive, two-way communication between mother and child. To use a metaphor, it's almost as if mother and infant can read each other's minds. We all know the expression that children pick up on everything. They do. From birth, a child possesses an exquisite sensitivity to a caregiver's tone of voice, facial expressions, eye movement, body language, and mood. We grown-ups tend to put a lot of value on the words we speak to each other. Children and infants can read all our other cues, which explains their uncanny ability to know what's *really* going on in a family.

Second, with attunement, the stakes are sky high for the infant. Attunement is his pipeline for his constant torrent of bids for attention, as he seeks approval from his lifeline, his caregiver. Psychiatrists at Cornell Medical School have used hours of videotape of mother-child interactions to study and analyze this subconscious "dance of rapport" between caregiver and child.[7] If the infant were to verbalize his bids, he might repeat, "Do you want me?...Do you want me now?...Do you still want me now?...How 'bout now?..." and so on. Every time his caregiver responds to his bids, the infant is reassured that his lifeline is intact and his survival is not threatened.

Nothing is more important to an infant than maintaining his caregiver's commitment to him.[8] That's why, even in the womb, infants make it their full-time job, 24/7, to monitor their caregiver's cues and remain constantly vigilant of her.

*In utero,* a fetus can analyze the chemistry of a mother's amniotic fluid, and he listens in on his mother's communication with other humans. After birth, babies know their mother's scent and are experts on even the most subtle glance, gesture, or tone of voice. Darwin himself described how infants keep detailed "files" on their mothers, because the only reality a child knows is that the mother-infant bond is essential to his survival. The infant depends on it for his survival, and he instinctively behaves so as to strengthen that connection.[9]

In some ways, attunement is a big part of what we call love. The complex give-and-take of attunement has all the tacit understanding and subtle, unconscious communication of other human relationships. For example, a caregiver coos at her baby in response to his squeal. Such affirming messages are sent back and forth roughly once every minute, as the caregiver mimics and matches the baby's level of emotion, which reassures the infant of being connected with his caregiver — his pipeline to survival.

But attunement not only ensures survival, it also gives him an identity of his own. It's by tuning in to the facial expressions, tone of voice, and body language of his first love, his mother, that an infant begins to get feedback about himself. A child's first glimmer of who he is comes from looking into his caregiver's face and noticing how she responds and reacts to him. This rapport creates the foundation for what will become his self-image.[10]

In sum, this attunement that occurs with the mother-infant bond serves several purposes: it inspires the caregiver to care for her infant, it helps the child survive and thrive, and their rapport is the child's first training in social skills. Attunement is like a nonstop, wordless conversation between parent and child, an interaction by which our children learn by osmosis. By interacting with their caregivers in this parent-child loop, babies soak up basic ground rules for interacting, such as how to be attentive and listen, how to start a conversation, how to read the other person's feelings, and other social graces that help us to interact with others as we grow up.[11]

Then, along comes weaning. Up to this point, you might say an infant has a captive audience with his caregiver, who is programmed to find him adorable, despite his occasional lack of social graces. But every infant arrives at a stage where he no longer turns exclusively to Mommy. The time when he begins to turn outward to others is the beginning of his emotional weaning process, the next step in his development.

## Weaning: A Crucial Step for a Child's Independence

I'm using "weaning" here in the broader sense: not weaning from breast milk, but emotional weaning from total dependence on the caregiver. As an infant develops, he begins to spend less time focusing exclusively on Mommy and turns more to others and the outside world. This is the beginning of his weaning process, as he gains some emotional independence and social experience.

Ideally, both caregiver and child are eager for increasing interactions with others — a mother with her peers, and a child with other kids. The mother-infant bond is obviously longer and more complex in humans than in other animals, but weaning is an essential stage of parenting that we share with all primates.

Weaning is a much more important transition than we realize. In fact, our emotional weaning as children affects our future personalities, our attitudes, and the way we interact in relationships. The smoother the transition from the mother-infant bond to independence, the better. But this transition is long, complex, and fraught with problems, some of which can be prevented. Let's look at common ways we as parents can inadvertently mess up that finely tuned balance between the mother-infant bond and weaning.

Jane Goodall, a famous primatologist, tells the following story about her research with chimpanzees in Africa:

Flo was the alpha female, the leader of her troop of chimpanzees. And it was Flo who tended to produce the strongest males. Almost every one of her offspring males went on to become the leader of the chimpanzee clan.

As Flo was getting a little older and slowing down, she gave birth to what turned out to be one of her last chimp babies, and Jane Goodall named him Flint. Flint and Flo became inseparable. Flint was always riding on Flo's back everywhere she went, and they seemed very close.

But what Jane Goodall noticed was that Flint remained on Flo's back a lot longer than most chimps do, even though Flo was slowing down with age. Usually there is a period of time during which a young chimp stops riding on his mother's back and walks on his own, as a move toward independence. Sometimes the mothers even push the chimps off their backs as if to say, "Hey, go get a life; get a job!" But with Flo and Flint things were different — they seemed to share a particularly close bond. They loved being together.

Unfortunately for Flint, he ended up paying a terrible price for that love. He had difficulty functioning within the group. He didn't exhibit the skills that he needed to function socially without his mother's intervention, and taking on a future leadership role seemed impossible. He seemed rather listless; unless he was with Flo, there was nothing for him to do. Flint seemed still attached to her somehow, even though he finally did get off her back.

The story ends with Flo finally dying. Flint went to the spot where she died and stayed with her corpse for weeks. He refused to eat; he refused to drink. Finally he died on that same site where his mother had died.

Now I guess you and I can look at that and say, "What a beautiful and touching story of love." But I would argue that Flint should have been on his way to a leadership position, and he died before he got that chance. And the conclusion that Jane Goodall drew was that something didn't go quite right in the weaning process.[12] No matter how many emotions humans may attach to it, the bottom line is that Flint didn't get a chance to do what he was supposed to be doing with his life.

So what does all that mean to you and me?

The story of Flo and Flint offers a clear example of what can happen when the mother and infant get stuck in their bond. Normally, the mother-infant bond should progress to independence as the infant is emotionally weaned. If the natural weaning process is disturbed, however, an Incomplete Weaning process can result in problems with the offspring's independence, as we saw with Flint. The same is true for humans.

The next sections unlock a key part of the unconscious, unhealthy process by which we neglect to wean our kids. First, we'll examine how parent and child can become stuck in the mother-infant bond. Then we'll examine how too much of the mother-infant bond and not enough weaning ends up programming a child for anxiety through attunement.

## How Caregiver and Child
## Become "Addicted" to Each Other

We have already discussed the primary hormones that contribute to the sense of well-being that makes the mother-infant bond last. The sense of well-being a caregiver and her infant feel when together can be attributed to the levels of oxytocin and other naturally occurring opiates in their brains. It's noteworthy that opiate levels are high in the brains of caregiver and child, as well as lovers, and of course drug addicts. The drug addict's opiates are artificial and ingested, but the opiates in loving relationships occur naturally. In fact, the cascades of natural opiates within two lovers greatly resemble the hormone patterns of caregiver and child.

Neuroscientist Jaak Panksepp theorizes that from the point of view of the brain, love is just like an addiction. The pleasure we feel from the rapport with our loved ones triggers the same neural circuits and releases the same hormones that an addict experiences when he does drugs. Even animals prefer to spend time with those animals that cause a burst of natural opiods or oxytocin in their brains — for example, animals with whom they've been playing, because play releases lots of "happiness" hormones. Therefore, we may conclude that these brain chemicals play a role in cementing our ties with loved ones.[13]

In a sense, one could say love is a wonderful addiction of the most exhilarating kind. But if the caregiver and child become too addicted to each other for too long, it can hamper weaning and lead to overattachment. That's a scenario where everyone in the family loses. Here's a real-life example:

Mike was an only child, and his mother always coddled him and treated him as special. She herself had grown up poor and sickly during the Depression, and she was determined to give him all the care, affection, and attention she felt she'd been deprived of. Mike was eight when she died of cancer, and her sisters took pity on the poor boy and showered him with more attention.

Unfortunately, Mike's transition into adulthood didn't go smoothly. Even into his forties, although Mike had a master's degree, he couldn't hold a job and lived with his father after his mother died. He had no friends, kept a dozen parakeets in their small apartment, and racked up staggering credit card debt. But when his father died, suddenly Mike got a job, and has been a dependable employee for over five years now. He's almost paid off all his debt, and he recently started dating an attractive woman.

Why did this man turn his life around, and learn independence at such a late age? Because he had to. Mike was coddled by his loving mother when he was young, but after her death, all his relatives (especially his father) pitied him and worried about him, so they took over the coddling: they loaned him money or set up job interviews for him, but he got nowhere. It was only when his back was up against the wall and it became too costly to ignore reality that he took charge of his life. Mike finally weaned himself because he ran out of "caregivers": first his mother, then his father died, and his other relatives grew too old to look after him. When there was no one left to overparent him, Mike had no choice but to step up.

As we saw with Ann and Nina at the beginning of this chapter, an anxious caregiver overcompensates. She wants to parent better than her parents did. She wants to make up for the "lack of love" she feels she had as a child. So she goes overboard. She puts too much energy into the mother-infant bond, showering the child with love and attention.

Given the decrease of informal get-togethers with friends and extended-family support we used to enjoy in previous generations, it's easy to get too caught up in the mother-infant bond. Also, if there's any tension in our marriages, sometimes it's easier to be with our kids than our spouse. Sure, kids make messes and throw tantrums, but they don't hold grudges or use passive-aggressive tactics like your spouse may (although some parents may wish to debate that!). Little kids are often more excited to see you, more affectionate, and more playful than your spouse. They know how to melt your heart with hugs and kisses. And after all, they're your flesh and blood.

Who wouldn't walk through fire for their kids? And how many couples do you know who are staying together for the kids' sake? With our kids, we hold the power; we get more affection, and they need us more.

It's tempting to get a little bit stuck in that bond, such that a caregiver becomes overinvolved with feeding, protecting, and giving too much attention to that child. It's almost as if she becomes addicted to her child and vice versa.

We have already seen how the mother-infant bond is a kind of hormonal addiction that ensures the infant's well-being. But if the caregiver doesn't actively wean the child from that primal bond, he remains addicted to it, and like any addiction, things get worse with time. For example, Flint the chimp's addiction cost him his leadership of the clan and, eventually, his life.

## Attunement:
## The Messenger of Escalating Anxiety

Without realizing it, this love-addicted parent with the best of intentions may (unknowingly) create her own worst nightmare, because coddling can impair a child's future independence and survival skills. Perhaps she infantilizes the child or overprotects him from mean kids on the playground. The subtle, unconscious message she is sending via their attunement pipeline is, "You can't handle this. Let me help you."

From birth a child trusts this tacit, attuned conversation with his mother (Mother knows best). So over time, the child may internalize that message in a kind of learned helplessness. This creates a vicious cycle where Mom's over-helpfulness programs a child to feel helpless, so the mother feels she has no choice but to help her child more.

Attunement is simply a sophisticated mechanism for communication between caregiver and child, but now it begins to deliver messages to the child that don't seem to jibe with Mommy's behavior. His caregiver may be verbally telling him to grow up, do well in school, and succeed, but the nonverbal messages he's receiving via attunement tell a very different story: "You can't handle this; let me take care of you."

It is exactly this incongruence between what parents say verbally and what they communicate through attunement that causes many problems for our children today. What we say to our kids doesn't matter nearly as much as what we worry about, because our worry is communicated much more clearly than we realize, via attunement. Everyone knows the old saying, "Kids pick up on everything," and it happens via attunement.

Attunement is only a messenger, but it's a perfectly honest and candid messenger, often communicating what we'd rather keep to ourselves. Attunement explains how we parents create a self-fulfilling prophecy in our children, and it starts off innocently enough. Here's how:

Parents often ask me, "What's the big deal if I still tie my kid's shoelaces?" In itself, of course, it's not a big deal, but it's seldom an isolated act.

Many of us worry about our child picking up emotional scars in childhood, and we want to minimize the trauma in our child's life, so we soothe him, instead of letting him learn to self-soothe. We worry about our kids' future: we want them to do well in school, go to top colleges, and succeed at their careers. So we help them with their homework. We worry whether our kids will become happy, fulfilled adults: we figure this starts with living joyful childhoods. Thus, we don't burden them with preparing meals, washing the dishes, or doing household chores. But we're completely unaware that our attunement is communicating one message, loud and clear: "I'm worried about this. You can't handle this, and you don't need to. Someone will take care of this for you."

Here's the definition of overparenting: it is doing for your child what your child can and should do for herself. Today's parents rescue our children from their anger or sadness. We rescue them from conflict or problem-solving. We use electronics to rescue them from boredom or loneliness, and we rescue them from feeding or cleaning up after themselves.

And we think we're preparing them for a successful launch into a happy adulthood?

Little things add up, such that children never learn the self-management skills they need to navigate adulthood. Mike's example above is, of course, an extreme one. But many of our children are ending up too dependent on their parents to soothe them and negotiate their lives for them.[14] Our worry shoots across the unspoken communication pipeline of attunement to our kids, and they have an increasing sense that something is wrong.

Things can escalate quickly. The caregiver's anxiety is transmitted through attunement to her son. He becomes more anxious and more helpless, which shoots more anxiety back to the caregiver. This increases her anxiety, and as she helps or rescues him she shoots even *more* anxiety back to him in the pipeline. This escalation continues until the child is so overloaded with anxiety that it hits critical mass: he develops a symptom or negative behavior, which of course *further* escalates his caregiver's anxiety. The caregiver may be increasingly alarmed that her child is becoming more helpless, and she has become too much of a caretaker of the child.

So beneath his awareness, the child is receiving mixed messages from their attunement: anxiety, a sense that something's wrong, and that he can't handle whatever it is. He's desperate to preserve the attunement lifeline that he's known since birth, but the anxiety he receives from it is becoming increasingly uncomfortable.

In the name of preserving the mother-infant bond, the child may become hypervigilant to his caregiver's every cue, to see if she's accepting or rejecting him. He will use any means to preserve her focus and attention. This includes positive behavior to please his caregiver or negative behavior that grabs her attention. He'll do anything, including behaving badly, feigning helplessness, or complaining of symptoms.

When we observe negative behavior in a child, we may wonder why he would engage in risky behavior that will likely be punished. But the negative behavior serves two purposes:

1. It's a cry for attention, forcing the child's caregiver to intensify the mother-infant bond to which the child is addicted.

2. The child's negative behavior is a defense mechanism. When his fragile nervous system hits "overload" with too much anxiety, his brain offloads that painful anxiety into a negative behavior or symptom as a way of coping with stress.

The child's trusted attunement has been sounding the alarm that something is wrong, and now his mind makes it so. The mind-body connection is a powerful force, and soon something *is* indeed wrong; either he begins an acting-out behavior, or else his mind manifests a symptom in his body.

So acting-out behavior or a symptom is not just a cry for attention; it's an indicator of the escalating anxiety shooting back and forth in the attunement pipeline between parent and child.

A child's attunement and addiction to his mom programs him to be more anxious in life. It is this anxious, unresolved emotional attachment we have with our parents that creates the level of chronic anxiety we carry into adulthood.[15] Because the child remains addicted to the mother-infant bond, he never ceases to be hypervigilant to his caregiver's every cue as a sign of her acceptance or rejection of him. On some level, he tends to overreact in his interactions with his caregiver: a very anxiety-producing pattern because he learns to always be focused on the other person, and on his guard.[16]

Earlier I playfully described Mommy as a child's first love, but there's more truth to that statement than we may think. As I said before, a big part of what we call love is attunement, and Mother Nature is highly efficient with the neurological systems she creates. The neurological paths in a mother's empathic response to her infant greatly resemble the paths activated when two lovers romance one another.[17] And it makes perfect sense: why create another neurosystem from scratch when you can borrow parts of an existing system? Attunement is the primary means of communication between lovers, as well as between caregiver and child. And because attunement is a child's training ground for how to interact with others, he will go on to replicate this anxiety-laden attunement in his future loving relationships.[18]

In summary, attunement is a candid messenger — perhaps too candid. It is the means by which a mother-infant bond that gets stuck then programs a child to become anxious and act out. This anxiety actually programs the child's brain for overreaction as he grows into an adult. The reason a caregiver and child's benign attunement can turn into such overreaction in the child is that the child has memories of the emotions he has experienced. As we'll see in the next section, the *amygdala* in our brain is keeping score.

## Our Brain's Amygdala:
## Once-Bitten, Twice-Shy

A part of our brain called the amygdala is the headquarters for our stress response. Our amygdala is like the "once bitten, twice shy" part of our brains, because it registers a memory of any "scar" from a stressful incident that occurs in the hope of avoiding the same pain twice. The problem is that any little mishap or hiccup in a caregiver's rapport with her infant may set off the alarms in the child's brain.

The infant is dependent on his caregiver for survival, so the stakes for each interaction are so high that it's easy for his amygdala to overreact. As we discussed earlier, attunement is a pipeline for a constant torrent of bids and responses between mother and child. It's both normal and inevitable that a caregiver cannot respond to all the child's bids. Perhaps Mommy was just tired or irritable when she didn't respond to her son's bid as part of their attunement, but the amygdala overreacts at the rejection: "Alert! Alert! Something's wrong! Potential abandonment by caregiver may be imminent!"

The child's brain resolves the situation as best it can, but unfortunately a poignant memory of that seemingly innocuous interaction has been recorded and may affect the child's reactions even into adulthood.

What makes this once-bitten, twice-shy amygdala a burden is that it essentially records a bunch of "misunderstandings" between caregiver and child back before the child could even speak. Thus, we all grow up with these wordless blueprints for how to react to others, but we don't understand where they came from or how they got there. Small wonder we are often surprised by what pushes our buttons, and our emotional outbursts seem to come out of nowhere. The amygdala recorded all these stressful memories back before our logical brain had any say in the matter. No one was guiding the amygdala to be reasonable and thoughtful. It simply sounded the alarm, believing the lifeline between caregiver and child was under threat, and then recorded anxious memories in the hope of reacting sooner next time to avoid any further threat.[19]

A New York University neuroscientist, Joseph LeDoux, has conducted research that helps us to understand the mechanics of why we overreact as adults. As infants, even before we learn to speak, our brain's amygdala is already hard at work, storing memories. If we overreact to something our caregiver does, or doesn't do, the amygdala records that incident and sensitizes us to watch out for future repeats. Our amygdala programs us to become hypervigilant and overreactive to a perceived slight by our caregiver. Note well that this is going on even before we learn to speak or have any conscious memories!

Unfortunately, the amygdala never forgets an insult, so we carry these anxious, hypervigilant, overreactive memories into our adult relationships. We then overreact to something our loved one says, and we can't explain why. We simply can't remember the original incident with Mommy that caused the amygdala to lay down its once-bitten, twice-shy warning in the first place, years ago.

The attunement between caregiver and infant is a nonstop, ongoing training for how the child will react in his future, adult relationships. It's amazing how a caregiver's subtle and minute cues are picked up by the child's sensitive attunement and then stored (often not accurately) in the amygdala of a developing child.

So Freud was right to point to the importance of childhood experiences in shaping our behaviors and thoughts as adults. But we parents have taken Freud too far and now we're missing the forest for the trees. We kill ourselves to provide perfect, trauma-free childhoods for our children, in the hope of minimizing our kids' nasty amygdala memories. But in fact, it is the anxiety we communicate via attunement that actually creates the scars on our amygdala.

As I said before, children pick up on everything. If we praise our children unceasingly and remove any criticism or unhappiness from their lives, that has little positive impact. It's our own worries and anxieties that are trumpeted to our child via our facial expressions, tone of voice, and the "vibe" of our attunement with our child. We parents may kid ourselves about what we're communicating, but our attunement never lies. We have to notice and manage what goes on in our heads — not so much what comes out of our mouths.

Our children "hear" our anxiety loud and clear via attunement, and it affects a kid's ability to regulate her emotions and self-soothe. Daniel Goleman refers to this as our "emotional thermostat."[20] For example, if a child gets upset, she may sense her parent is upset that she's upset, especially if we rush to soothe her and take away the pain. It's as if we parents are saying (via attunement), "You don't have to regulate your emotions; I'll do it for you, by protecting you and removing trauma from your childhood."

Thus overparenting hampers the development of a child's emotional thermostat, by denying the child the opportunity to learn how to self-soothe. Every chance the child misses to exercise and develop his own emotional thermostat will cost him dearly in the long run.

For example, don't worry that disciplining your kid will traumatize her. Instead, create more intimacy with your spouse and manage the anxiety within yourself so that you'll be more inclined to wean, and less likely to overparent, your kid in a thousand subtle ways. This matters much more than whether your child stomps and cries during a time-out, and we'll examine this in later chapters. In the next section of this chapter, we'll examine how the hypervigilance and overreaction we create in our overattachment to our kids eventually shows up in their adult relationships.

## The Child Replays This Drama as an Adult

So what does our amygdala and attunement mean for weaning our children? If the negative programming of our infant brain is inevitable, what difference does weaning make?

It's a question of degree. Over time, there's no doubt this pattern of hypervigilance becomes entrenched, such that the child is hardwired for chronic anxiety. But we can influence how much hypervigilance our child has for her caregiver. A child who is smoothly weaned from her natural addiction to her caregiver will carry less chronic anxiety for the rest of her life.

As I said in the introduction to this book, we're not aiming for perfection here. If good weaning for a child can reduce the amount of overreaction in our child's adult relationships, over time that might make the difference between the child having a divorce or a marriage that lasts. Over a lifetime, it could mean the difference between a flourishing career and a dead-end job. Weaning our children gives parents the opportunity to maximize their child's potential for a happy life. Good weaning will have more impact in the long run than most of the areas that parents currently focus their energy on, like their child's lessons, sports clubs, or extra help at math.

It's a natural process in many animals for the parent to wean her offspring, and it's the offspring's job to protest. Think of it as life's first negotiating process: each party has her self-interests, and there are a series of aggressive and conciliatory tactics employed to try and get what each wants.

Jane Goodall documented this same resistance to weaning in chimps and relates a case in point drawn from the life of one of the Gombe chimps, Fifi's four-year-old son, Frodo. Frodo was in the process of being weaned and well on his way toward perfecting the art of the tantrum. One day, when his mother no longer allowed him to ride on her back, he followed behind, whimpering. Suddenly he started to scream loudly while staring at the side of the trail. His mother sprang into action and tossed him on her back for safety, although Goodall saw no sign there was actually a threat. After she had witnessed several of these encounters, Goodall concluded that these offspring were deliberately manipulating their mothers. They did not want to wean from their addiction to their mothers' comfort, and they were willing to use any tactic to maintain that addiction.[21]

If our child were addicted to drugs, of course we'd take him to rehab. For a child addicted to the mother-infant bond, emotional weaning is the cure. Freud referred to Incomplete Weaning as unresolved emotional attachment or transference, because we tend to transfer this hypersensitivity to Mommy into our adult relationships. Psychiatrist Murray Bowen called it fusion, because it's as if parent and child remain fused together emotionally, never having separated properly. The child may grow up physically, but emotionally his weaning and development are incomplete.

For example, a rebellious teen is often especially addicted emotionally to his mother, although it may appear to be the opposite. His arguments or his distancing are simply a clumsy fight-or-flight response as he attempts to break his addiction to the mother-infant bond and establish his own identity. In fact, most of a rebellious teen's beliefs are not carefully thought-out principles. He often just creates opposing beliefs to those of his parents, in a clumsy attempt to overcome his addiction and become an independent self.

Let's look again at Ann and Nina from the beginning of this chapter: Even after Ann poured so much love into her daughter, the girl still felt insecure and unloved. Neither party realized this, but Ann could *never* satisfy Nina's need for love, because Nina was addicted to the mother-infant bond and needed more and more. The lack of emotional weaning between them meant that Nina and her mother were so emotionally wrapped up in each other that there were no boundaries to define realistic expectations between them.

As Nina became increasingly anxious, believing she wasn't getting what she needed, her attunement with Ann went

awry and became a misattunement, full of misunderstandings, overreactions, and unspoken bitterness.

Nina felt strongly that Ann *should* know what to give to
make Nina feel better, but her mother had let Nina down, at
least in Nina's eyes. Hence her resentment and estrangement
from her mother.

Nina couldn't articulate it at the time, but she had a sense
of the emotional burden this relationship had put on her
all through her childhood: "After all I've done to support
her, why couldn't she come through for me in *my* time of
need?" was the unspoken subtext of her relationship with
her mother during her teens.

So as a teen, she rebelled and took revenge on her mother
by cutting off from her and starting to hang out with a bad
crowd to gain their approval. Ironically, she ended up feeling
even *more* preoccupied with not receiving enough love than
her mother had felt in relation to her own mother.

As many parents of teenagers will attest, a rebellious teenager has an uncanny knack for probing and poking a parent's
insecurities. That's because the teenager has been so emotionally wrapped up with her parent for so long that she truly
*does* know where the parent is sensitive. So the teen pushes
her parent's buttons, and the parent reacts in an immature
manner. Then the teenager retaliates, and so it escalates.
They both blame each other, but each is just as caught up
in this dance of emotional reactivity via their oversensitive,
overreacting attunement.

As these rebellious teens grow into adults and roughly
"tear" themselves from their parents as best they can, their
addiction to the mother-infant bond duplicates itself in adult
relationships. They cannot escape their chronic anxiety, so

the intimate relationship is the Achilles heel of these people, because they overreact to their lover's cues, and yet they cannot help being lured back into the addiction of love.[22]

As I mentioned earlier in the chapter, Mother Nature is highly efficient with the neurological systems she creates, and the neuropathways of a starstruck lover's brain resemble those of a caregiver and child in the grips of the mother-infant bond. Freud picked up on the similar behaviors of mother-child love and the affection of two lovers a hundred years ago, and neuroscience now confirms it. We duplicate the patterns of our "first love" with our caregiver in our subsequent relationships.[23]

Now we can understand why we have drama in our intimate relationships. If we are not sufficiently weaned emotionally as children, our attunement to our mothers becomes too intense and too sensitive. When we bring that same level of attunement to our intimate relationships, we are transferring that oversensitivity to our loved ones as well. That's Freud's concept of *transference* in spades.

Unfortunately, the same is true for our own children. As stated above, the child's anxious, hypervigilant, intense relationship with his caregiver becomes entrenched over time. His amygdala is programmed to expect the worst, and his hypervigilance to the cues of other people primes him to overreact, thereby increasing his susceptibility to his loved one's emotions.[24]

In other words, because he has been so focused on the caregiver, the child's intense focus becomes a pattern in all his future relationships, as implied in such expressions as a "Madonna Complex," "Mama's Boy," or "Daddy's Little Girl."

His focus on his caregiver becomes more generally a "focus on other," especially with future partners. It becomes uncomfortable to be in a relationship — very intense and volatile — and his clingy-ness may drive others away. If such a person does succeed in sustaining a relationship, he forms the kind of love-addiction we described earlier, where he's anxious and obsessive about the relationship. He may become jealous or fear abandonment.[25]

## Summary: How and Why
## We Pass Our Baggage On to Our Kids

To summarize, I hope the above section has helped you begin to understand one reason we have drama in our relationships. The quality of our weaning from the mother-infant bond plays a role in determining how anxious we become as adults in our relationships. And the less we were weaned from that primal bond, the more addicted and hypervigilant to Mommy we remained. Each of us falls somewhere on a continuum of Incomplete Weaning, so there's no such thing as the perfect weaning. We may be tempted to blame our parents or ourselves, but our weaning, whether more or less complete, is a process that goes on beneath our awareness, so it's nobody's fault.

Understanding the mother-infant bond, attunement, and weaning are crucial to how we parent our children, because now we know how, and why, we pass our baggage on to our kids. In order to better wean our children, we have to let go of the #1 myth in parenting today: the more attention we give our kids, the better they'll turn out. Today many believe the popular myth that our suffering as adults stems from a lack of parental attention when we were kids. Many parents have come to take this myth for granted, without even questioning it.

I believe that today we parents are trying too hard. We are trying too hard to give kids everything, and show them everything, and spend all our time with them. We have the best of intentions, but we're playing with fire if we mess with a child's process of gaining independence. We need to stop trying to give our children the perfect childhood, because they need to learn how to self-soothe and self-regulate their own emotions. As psychologist and author Daniel Goleman writes,

> More important for a child than seeking some elusive perpetual happiness, researchers find, is learning how to de-escalate emotional storms. . . . Given how the brain masters social resilience, children need to rehearse for the difficulties of social life, not experience a steady monotone of delight. When a child gets upset, the value lies in attaining some mastery over that reaction.[26]

There is no substitute for the hard knocks of the playground. It trains us for the office politics and the family squabbles of adult life. The hard knocks we face as children are the ideal training ground for social resilience, because in childhood upsets, the stakes are low and children can experiment in how to handle themselves. It helps to prepare them for adulthood, where the stakes are much higher in relationships.[27]

At some point, someone in your family has to declare, "I'm not going to pass my family's baggage on to my kids. I'm not interested in blame, I'm interested in learning how to deal with this incomplete weaning pattern, so that the legacy can stop with me." Someone has to say, "The buck stops here." My question is: Will it be you?

In parenting, the stakes are very high. We truly are shaping the lives of our future generations. We need to become painfully aware of how some of our "child-friendly" practices are in fact not child-friendly at all. And we need to understand the price our child will pay if we dodge our own marriages.

We claim that we cater to children's needs out of love for them, but I think sometimes it's to avoid our own discomfort. If our marriage is uncomfortable, we prefer to spend time with our kids and focus on their needs. If our children badger us with their demands, we don't want to feel uncomfortable, so we give in. We want to be their friends, not their parents.

But our kids don't need more friends; they need a parent who's not afraid to be a parent, and not afraid to be married.

To raise happy kids, put your marriage first.

We must regain a balance between tending our marriages and nurturing our children. When our marriages meet our intimacy needs, then we can stop marrying our children. This frees up our kids to build their own identity, learn self-reliance, and become happy, independent adults who pursue their passions in life. Our marriage can also set a great example for their future relationships. It's win–win for every member of the family.

But please remember to be gentle with yourself as you grapple with your family's legacy. We can't attain perfection in one generation. You don't have to hit any home runs; a few base hits will be just fine. And if you ever get discouraged, remember that all you have to do is do a little better than your parents did. Even if you receive no medal for it, your efforts will transform your children's lives and the lives of their future generations.

This work will be your finest hour.

In the next chapters, we'll learn what causes an unhappy marriage that can contribute to the unhappy kids described above. Basically, your fight-or-flight response controls much more of your daily behavior than you realize, and it may be playing havoc with your marriage. Blaming your spouse stems from your fight response, and distancing from your spouse stems from your flight response. The sooner you become aware of how your fight-or-flight response is working against your marriage, the sooner you can turn things around for your kids — and your marriage.

# Part 2

## HOW WE HURT OUR MARRIAGES,
## WHICH HURTS OUR KIDS

# Chapter Three

# Why We Hurt
# Those We Love Most

Bob and Jackie are attending his company's annual barbeque. Bob runs into an office mate, who cryptically mentions seeing a deeply disturbing letter about Bob's job performance at work. When he hears this news, Bob gets anxious. He's trying to have fun at the dinner, but his worry starts getting the best of him. What could be in that letter that is so deeply disturbing?

Jackie is collecting their kids, and preparing them to go home. She's in that "gotta get home" mode. She's tired, and the kids are cranky. Bob shows up at the doorway of the room and says, "I need a few minutes to talk to my office mate."

Jackie doesn't say a word, but she rolls her eyes and sighs with dismay, and that gesture just nails Bob. In the flash of an instant he feels, "Here we go *again*. She's upset again."

From Bob's point of view, the first shot has already been fired, even though Jackie never said a word. Bob fires back with, "You have no idea what I'm up against! So just take the kids and the car and go home!"

Bob then goes to talk with his office mate. Jackie actually does wait for Bob, so they go home together, but the evening is less than relaxing. There's a lot of silence and tension between them. A few skirmishes break out between them; they blame each other.

Jackie thinks to herself, "Why was Bob yelling at me like that? If it's a work problem, why is he taking it out on me?"

And Bob in turn thinks to himself, "Why did she have to give me that ticked-off look at the barbeque? I'm doing the best I can! Doesn't she trust me that if I say I need a few minutes that it must be for some good reason? Can't she see that I'm not just running off to the casino or something?"

You may have guessed at this point that this argument is not about thoughtful responses. Bob and Jackie are stuck in what I call Blaming Your Spouse.

There are three ways that couples deal with tension in their marriages: Projection onto Our Children, Blaming Our Spouse, and Distancing from Our Spouse. This chapter examines Blaming Our Spouse and helps answer the question, "What causes a good marriage to go bad, and how can we avoid it?"

Before we examine Blaming Our Spouse, it is essential to grasp a key concept in both this chapter and the next: the fight-or-flight response. This response controls much more of your daily behavior than you might realize, and until you recognize and deal with it, it will play havoc with your marriage on a daily basis. I will discuss manifestations of fight or flight in two ways. In this chapter, we will examine how blame stems from the "fight" part of the fight-or-flight response. Distancing from Our Spouse is the "flight" part of the fight-or-flight response, which we'll take up in the next chapter.

This chapter on blame covers three essential points:

1. We don't realize we're "trigger-happy" — that is, every day we overreact to our spouses and trigger our fight response — which includes not only arguing but also *criticizing*.

2. We believe our criticism of our spouse is accurate, but we don't realize we're often just spraying our own anxiety onto our spouse by scapegoating.

3. A common pattern leading to a troubled spouse or child is when one spouse becomes dominating and blaming, while the other spouse becomes submissive and self-blaming.

These points are crucial because we may currently believe we see our relationships quite objectively; in essence, our perception seems to be "the truth." In fact, the way we view our loved ones is much more subjective than we realize. Blaming is actually a manifestation of the human instinct to "offload" anxiety onto others in the form of scapegoating. Once you begin to notice that your criticism is often actually just your anxious irritability talking, you can nip your fight response in the bud more often.

The goal of this chapter is to help you reduce the tension in your marriage caused by blame. Learning which type of blamer you are — whether self- or other-blaming — will help you spot the blaming pattern when you are in the midst of its control. This awareness will help you loosen its grip over your behavior, so you can catch yourself in the early stages of your fight response and defuse it.

Changing your own perceptions is easier than the frustrating dead-end of trying to change your spouse's behavior anyway! It's much more empowering to learn how to manage your own anxiety, because that way you can take responsibility for *you* — whether the people around you choose to improve or not.

## We Don't Realize We're "Trigger-Happy"

In our example above, Bob's first reaction was not to what Jackie said but to her facial expression. He may or may not have interpreted it correctly. But he was already anxious and irritable given the bad news from his work colleague. He was primed for blaming his spouse. Was he accurate about what Jackie's expression meant, or did he unfairly jump to conclusions?

Actually, it doesn't matter. Blaming Your Spouse is simply our fight-or-flight instinct run amok. When we react instinctively to a real or imagined threat, any sense of subtle nuance flies out the window. The fight-or-flight response is the body's emergency stress response, with the sole purpose of removing the threat as quickly as possible. So our brain commandeers all operations, and shuts down any nuanced thinking that might confuse or slow down our reaction time.

We are left only with tunnel vision and snap judgments, so we can see things only in black-and-white, e.g., "I'm 100 percent in the right, and that person is attacking me. I must defend. That *other* person has created the threat, and I have no choice but to react." When we're in the grip of fight or flight, our brain is so flooded with adrenaline that we cannot see any role we played in creating the threat. We can only conquer or flee (more on flight in chapter 4).

It's as if our brain is on autopilot. In our fight response, our anxious irritability takes over our brains and convinces us that some threat is imminent, so we're primed to overreact, and anything can set us off. We may not even realize how we are actually picking a fight with our spouse when we criticize him or her.

Have you ever noticed how, when you're in a bad mood, everything seems to go wrong and your spouse seems to be acting like a jerk? Your "bad mood" is simply another name for your anxious irritability, which predisposes you to perceive your spouse as acting like a jerk and provoking you. You believe he deserves your attack because you think of it as a counterattack. When a couple quibbles about who started the fight, chances are your spouse probably perceives *you* as having fired the first shot, and therefore he feels justified in *his* "counterattack." That's how things escalate when we're in the grip of the black-and-white tunnel vision of fight or flight. Your bad mood often *precedes* how people treat you, even though you think of it as the result of *their* behavior.

Do you have any doubt that anxiety or irritability floods your mind every day and primes your fight response? Imagine that you hooked yourself up to a biofeedback machine that measures your brain waves, blood pressure, skin temperature, sweat, heartbeat, and the presence of stress hormones like cortisol. You'd be amazed at how high these levels are as you think about various issues in your life, even when you consider yourself to be calm. So are the biofeedback instruments lying, or are we simply unaware of how often our bodies are in fight-or-flight mode?

The anxious irritability of our "bad mood" can make us trigger-happy, shooting off our fight-or-flight response too quickly. Most of us have noticed that we are much more easily provoked if we're already irritated by something else.

It's as if stress primes us for anger, because our brain releases stress hormones in our brains, which puts our fight-or-flight response on Red Alert. That's why, if we had a tough day at the office, we're much more likely to get upset if the kids make too much noise when we get home.[1]

That's what is happening in Bob's head when he snaps at Jackie for her facial expression in our earlier example. His stress response has already been mobilized by his work colleague's news about the letter, so he is now particularly easy to upset. Almost anything will provoke him; he's trigger-happy.

In fairness to Bob, we can't say that Jackie's eye-rolling was exactly a neutral response. Even though she said nothing, she communicated contempt quite clearly,[2] and contempt is a particularly potent form of Blaming Your Spouse. But the point is not who started it between Bob and Jackie, because it's not just about this event. As we saw in chapter 2, it's about an accumulation of amygdala memories of past skirmishes, which heighten their stress response when they're around each other and thus prime them to overreact.

People in a troubled marriage believe their spouse's seemingly bad behavior justifies the blame they feel toward their spouse. They can't see how their own anxiety may have contributed to their irritability, which in turn colored their negative perception of their spouse's behavior. This pattern can become a vicious circle, where irritability evokes blame, which in turn evokes more irritability, and so on, in a downward spiral that sours the marriage.

Many people tend to see their relationships and conflicts as random and accidental, almost as if "fate" acted on them. In fact, *many aspects* of conflict in our relationships are predictable, repetitive, and within our control. Imagine the power it would unleash if you could control even a *fraction* more of your relationships. It is beneficial to consider how our fight response may play a role in our marital conflicts.

What sets you and your partner off? His table manners? The way you squeeze the toothpaste? My wife and I tend to blow up over little things. Then we blame each other for getting upset over such a little thing. Big drama can follow.

But here's the rub: during the argument, we may have felt justified in our anger, but in retrospect it seems so trivial that we cannot understand why it upset us so much. If an outsider asked us about the substance of our fight, we'd likely feel sheepish to respond. This invites the question: If we were indeed seeing things as objectively as each of us thought, why the big drama over small issues? If our eyes weren't clouded by anger and fear, why did two intelligent people escalate so quickly over such a trifle?

Psychiatrist Michael Kerr confirms the old joke about our spouses: can't live with 'em, can't live without 'em. Couples who argue may often threaten to leave the marriage, but there's an intense love/hate addiction to each other that somehow draws them back together time and again: "Conflictual mates are generally very 'stuck' to one another. Their relationship is like an exhausting, draining, and strongly invigorating roller coaster ride; people threaten never to buy another ticket, but they usually do."[3]

Whenever there's tension, conflict, or just silence in a marriage, both spouses tend to believe it's mostly (if not completely) the other spouse's fault. In my role as a minister, I often hear divorcees describe their ex-partners, saying, "We grew apart," or "We had different interests." In my experience, what they really mean is, "I outgrew my spouse." Sometimes people will complain for hours about what is wrong with their ex-spouses without ever stopping to consider what that says about their own maturity level in choosing a spouse or their own role in that failed relationship.

## Scapegoating:
## Spraying Our Anxiety onto Others

We humans tend to think we have a clear, unbiased, true view of the world, and of the people around us. That couldn't be further from the truth. We view the world through fight-or-flight glasses. These glasses have very thick, cloudy lenses — one lens is anger; the other is fear. When our fight response gives us black-and-white tunnel vision, what we perceive suddenly seems like certain reality to us. It is that disconnection between our perception and objective reality that creates much of the drama we experience in relationships.

It is quite remarkable how little objectivity we really have. Humans may wear nice suits and speak sophisticated words, but when it comes to how we behave in relationships, we might as well be naked in the jungle again, screaming and swinging from tree to tree. For example, what we refer to as "office politics" is just another name for the herd instinct, territoriality, and the fight-or-flight response. In our cave man days, these fight-or-flight glasses kept us ever vigilant against the dangers of the jungle. But in our modern lives, our fight-or-flight glasses force us, often inappropriately, to treat life as though "it's a jungle out there."

When things aren't going our way in the jungle of life, our frustration increases, which in turn increases our anxious irritability. Unfortunately, one of our most tempting outlets for this irritability is Blaming Our Spouse. In fact, it's instinctive.

Neuroscience has proven that the human brain is hardwired to "scapegoat," and it's a trait we share with many other species. Scapegoating is an ancient defense mechanism in the brain to offload our anxious reactivity onto someone nearby. From a survival-of-the-fittest perspective, this is a valuable adaptation. The more of our anger we can offload onto others, the easier it is for us to pursue our own desires and compete for scarce resources.[4]

In our example above, Jackie's desire is to get home to the nest and put her brood to bed. Bob's desire is to get some resolution with his colleague regarding this disturbing letter. Their "competition for resources" is for one car to get home in. But clearly, both go on to blame each other for their negative feelings, and each believes the other started it. Both are overreacting to the situation because their anxious irritability is already aroused. They are primed for blame.

In a sense, many spouses are stuck in fight-or-flight mode and unconsciously seek someone to fight with (or flee from). People with higher anxiety perceive more threats in their lives more often and tend to act as if they're in life-and-death situations when, objectively speaking, they are not. If both spouses have a high level of anxiety, they will have a greater tendency to attack or avoid each other.

Best-selling author, psychologist, and primatologist Frans de Waal, in his book *Our Inner Ape*, describes our tendency to blame others as a displacement of aggression:

It's undeniable that scapegoating is one of the most basic, most powerful, least conscious psychological reflexes of the human species, one shared with so many other animals that it may well be hardwired. . . . The quintessential example is pain-induced aggression in rats. Place two rats on an iron grid through which they are given an electric shock, and the moment they feel the pain they attack each other.[5]

Of course, blaming others for our suffering is nothing new. The term "scapegoat" derives from Hebrew, denoting an ancient Jewish ritual of atonement during Yom Kippur. The ritual involved two goats. One was sacrificed as a symbolic "payment" to God for the people's sins. The other goat (the "escape goat") was driven into the wilderness, symbolically carrying the sins of the people on his back. This was how people freed themselves from their suffering, which they believed was brought about by their sins. That's why today a scapegoat usually refers to an innocent person who is blamed for the suffering or wrongdoing of others.[6]

Neither spouse is aware of it in our example, but Bob is shifting his work problem about the disturbing letter onto his wife. Jackie is shifting her problem with cranky kids and her fatigue onto Bob. Their scapegoating doesn't help either problem, but when we're already primed to overreact, we can't stop ourselves.

Blaming Our Spouse is a vicious circle that can become a downward spiral that sours our marriages. It starts with anxious irritability that makes us trigger-happy with our fight response. Next, we either provoke, or feel provoked by, our spouse, so we unleash what we perceive to be a counterattack. This either simmers as tension between the couple, or escalates into open conflict. Either way, it creates an amygdala memory that leaves both spouses even more reactive to each other the next time around.

## Blamers and Self-Blamers

There are two types of blamers: those who usually blame their spouses, and those who usually blame themselves for what goes wrong in their marriage. Bob and Jackie are an example of blaming each other.

Many of us go through life with a simple belief: when we get angry at someone, our anger is of course justified. Benjamin Franklin put it well: "Anger is never without a reason but seldom a good one."[7] We don't see ourselves as being judgmental or projecting onto that person; we believe anyone in our situation would feel the same way. We also seldom see ourselves as critical. Instead, we imagine, we're accurately pointing out someone else's faults, and we think any reasonable person would agree on that person's faults.

Let's assume our perspective is in fact true, and we're always right. This puts us in a tricky position, because it means we can never be at peace. There will always be some darn person saying or doing the wrong thing and causing us to get upset. As long as our peace of mind depends on the behavior of people around us, how can we win?

If we're not in control of our own emotions, i.e., if other people are the cause of our upset, then our only option is to hang around people we can control or else retreat from social contact. Neither option is a desirable lifestyle for most of us.

What can couples do to step out of their vicious cycle of irritability and blame? Blamers need to recognize that conflict is almost never black and white. When they criticize, the fault they are pointing out is only part of the story. They may already be anxious about something else, which primes them to overreact to their spouses. If blamers can begin to wonder whether they're seeing things objectively, they can sometimes catch themselves before they put on their tunnel-vision glasses and head down the road to scapegoating. Now let's look at some examples of a blamer married to a self-blamer.

The night before their big trip abroad, Vicky told her husband that she'd left just enough milk in the fridge for his breakfast cereal. Her husband got up the next morning, ate his cereal, and they departed for the airport — only to get stuck in horrendous traffic. As they worried about missing their plane, Vicky mused out loud, "If I hadn't mentioned the milk, you wouldn't have had breakfast, and we wouldn't be late."

Her husband responded, "You always nag me to eat breakfast, so I did what you told me to do."

◆ ◆ ◆

Gail and her husband, Alan, both work as teachers. They recently decided to place their one-year-old daughter in day-care, and on the first day, she tripped and injured her arm. Gail immediately beat herself up for choosing the wrong day-care program and noted that the pants she had put on her daughter were a bit too long. Alan didn't try to talk her out of blaming herself, because he too was harboring thoughts that perhaps this could have been avoided.

◆ ◆ ◆

Alexis is an executive at a Fortune 500 company, but she feels guilty that she often gets home long after her husband and two daughters. She makes dinner for her family and apologizes profusely for overcooking the steak as she puts the food on the table. Her husband says, "I can't even cut this! Were you on the phone while you were cooking?"

◆ ◆ ◆

In couples with a blamer and a self-blamer, the blamer will be outspoken and critical in blaming the other, and the self-blamer will be introverted and self-critical, tacitly agreeing that his or her spouse must be right, or even shouldering the blame outright.

Self-blamers tend to marry other-blamers. The question is: Why would anyone actively choose to suffer like that? Nobody makes such a choice consciously. As we will discuss in chapter 6, we unconsciously feel chemistry for a mate with a similar level of anxiety. I'm using "anxiety" in a broad sense here — not just the anxiety that causes us to worry, but also a more primal anxiety that determines how we respond when we encounter stressful situations. Chemistry attracts us to others with similar anxiety levels, but that anxiety can be expressed in very different behaviors. So the high-anxiety self-blamer may instinctively find an equally high-anxiety blamer to match. Frans de Waal observes:

> I've heard women say that this is a male thing, that women tend to internalize blame, whereas men have no compunction about finding others at fault. Men prefer to give rather than get ulcers. It's depressing to learn that we share this tendency — which creates so many

innocent victims — with rats, monkeys, and apes. It's a deeply ingrained tactic to keep stress at bay at the expense of fairness and justice.[8]

This may be one of those moments where you should take a deep breath as you read this. Facing the human tendency to blame and scapegoat is ugly, and it goes against our sense of justice. But I hope it's a relief at least to confront the problem squarely. By becoming aware of this innate tendency to blame, hopefully it will soften our tendency to blame others. And maybe it will give us a little more compassion if we begin to blame ourselves or someone blames us. Forgive them, for they know not what they do.

## A Common Pattern
## Leading to a Troubled Spouse or Child

The blaming/self-blaming pattern described above can be very toxic to a family. For example, imagine a couple where the husband is very dominating, while the wife is more passive and bumbling, under the blamer's scrutiny. Over the years, this pattern may intensify. He may run the household with an iron fist, while she becomes more dysfunctional, perhaps to the point of developing depression or a psychosomatic illness. This type of couple rarely argues, although a visitor may feel uncomfortable around them because the blamer speaks so critically and harshly to the self-blamer. For example, I'm amazed by the number of families I observe where one parent is a bully and the other parent is passive and compliant.

It may be tempting to judge the bully as bad and the seemingly passive victim as innocent, but that's missing the point. Both spouses are responsible for the roles they play in the marriage, even if they took on their role without their awareness. Therefore, neither person is more to blame than the other. It truly does take two to tango — a painful symbiosis that neither can easily transcend.

Why would two spouses engage in such a painful dance? One could say that, in an unhealthy way, they *need* each other. The anxiety and insecurities of a blaming spouse may cause him to take on a dominant, decisive role, to overcompensate for how unsure he feels about himself. And the self-blamer reinforces her spouse's dominance by displaying a more helpless, indecisive image because she feels anxious and unsure of herself.

Ironically, even as a self-blaming spouse tends to perceive her partner as critical and judgmental, she actually evokes that behavior from him. For every action there is an equal and opposite reaction. We make these kinds of demands on our spouses unconsciously; it's like an instinctive "black market" of vigorous emotional trading that goes on beneath the surface of our marriages. Hence, the paradox that the blamer looks good and the self-blamer looks bad, but inside they both feel equally insecure and anxious. Most of our marriages are not that extreme, but we all share the same anxious tendency to blame our spouse or allow our spouse to join us in blaming ourselves — it's just a matter of degree.

Though this power struggle goes on constantly, there are no winners in terms of maturity or happiness. That's the problem when our fight-or-flight instincts run our marriage.

We may think of ourselves as independent, freethinking individuals. Sadly, that is true only a tiny percentage of the time. Most of the time, we perceive ourselves as victims even as we're attacking our spouse.

In our example of Vicky and her husband being late for their flight, they both play a role. It's not as if their marriage was utopic until her husband woke up one day and started blaming her. If Vicky already has a tendency to blame herself for things gone wrong, then she may have unwittingly set a precedent. In order for Vicky's husband to blame her for things that are not her fault, his wife has to allow herself to become a victim of her blaming husband. To suggest that she has no power or intelligence to stand up to her husband is to minimize her.

Likewise, we shouldn't dismiss her as foolish to have picked such a mean spouse in the first place. First, he probably represented himself better during courtship. Second, if we find ourselves feeling no attraction toward nice guys, it's not as if we can *force* ourselves to feel chemistry for them. Vicky couldn't help the powerful, primal chemistry that drew her to her husband like a magnet, to complete each other, as we'll discuss in chapter 6 on chemistry.

Here's why the blamer-and-self-blamer couples often end up with a troubled spouse or child: in a conflictual marriage where two blamers argue often, it's less likely that one of them will develop physical or emotional symptoms. In a sense, the spouses each "stand up for themselves," because each spouse is convinced that it is the other spouse who needs to do the changing. But in a marriage between a blamer and a self-blamer, both spouses essentially agree that it is one spouse who needs to do the changing: the self-blamer. On the surface, this marriage may seem calmer because there is less verbal conflict. But when the blame and criticism are moving mostly in one direction, the recipient of that blame may develop symptoms.[9]

In a sense, then, arguing is not always such a bad thing. There is no question that it can be unpleasant, but at least both spouses are emotionally engaged with each other, and they are both standing up for what they believe in. In a funny way, it doesn't matter who is right. It only matters that the spouses are addressing touchy topics head-on in their marriage. When it comes to sustaining a long-term relationship, arguing may be the least of all evils. We can learn to argue more constructively if we practice noticing how our anxiety fuels our irritability. Just becoming a touch more aware of our irritability will make us slightly less volatile in tense conversations, so things won't escalate as rapidly in an argument.

The solution for the couples with one self-blamer is the same as for the couples who blame each other. The blamer needs to begin to recognize that his criticism is his own anxiety talking, manifested as irritability. His anxiety predisposes him to be trigger-happy, which primes him to blame and scapegoat at the slightest provocation. The self-blamer needs to recognize that she's not seeing things objectively either. She, too, has high levels of anxiety that also predispose her to blame, although she unfortunately tends to default to self-blame. Let's look at an example of a couple who began defusing a chronic conflict by recognizing their roles as blamers.

## Less Drama, More Control

Ginny thought her husband, Rob, was too strict with their nine-year-old son, Owen, at mealtimes. Rob would scold Owen for placing his milk glass too close to the edge of the table, because it risked spilling. And one time, Owen spilled his pasta on the floor and Rob made him pick it up, wash it, and eat it all. Owen was in tears, but when Ginny told Rob he was too harsh, Rob vehemently disagreed and things escalated into yet another argument on the subject.

When they brought this issue up with me, at first Ginny was sure that Rob was to blame for their chronic, polarized conflict. But as we discussed it, she began to see there was a strange triangle between Ginny, Rob, and Owen.

Ginny felt Rob was generally too strict with Owen, and she saw Rob as the "Bad Cop" in their family. So perhaps she was too lenient with Owen in other instances, because she felt sorry for Owen as the victim of his mean dad. She became the "Good Cop." Owen began to look to her for protection whenever Rob disciplined him, and maybe sometimes she was too quick to defend Owen. This defense in turn undercut Rob's authority with Owen and polarized both parents.

In the meantime, she had to admit that Owen's table manners weren't exactly stellar.

Once a conflict becomes stuck in two polarized positions, where each spouse blames the other for the problem they face, the only way out is for each spouse to notice their anxiety. Rob noticed that he had been spoiled as a child and was anxiously overreacting to Owen's bad habits because he was intent on "making sure his son didn't end up like him." On the other hand, Ginny was trying to be friends with her son. Consequently, she was perhaps a little lax on discipline, which left Owen with some bad habits.

In a sense, by playing Good Cop with Owen, Ginny contributed to Rob's playing Bad Cop because he felt obliged to straighten out Owen's bad habits that Ginny had let slide.

In other words, it's never as simple as "Ginny is right, and Rob is wrong." It's often very difficult to objectively discern who's "right," and it actually doesn't matter anyway. What matters is that if one or both spouses can begin to see how their anxious irritability is playing a role in a chronic conflict, they can soften the rigid, extreme positions they've taken and find some compromise in the middle.

As soon as spouses begin to understand that Blaming (whether of the other spouse or of themselves) is merely a symptom of their own underlying anxiety, they can begin to make progress. It's a two-part process. First, one person begins to recognize that anxiety dictates more of her irritability, judgment, and criticism of her spouse than she realized. This is an insight, because up until now she firmly believed that she was objectively viewing what a jerk her spouse was, and that any reasonable person would see him the same way. She believed she was seeing "truth" rather than perceptions colored by her bias.

The second part of making progress occurs when this same person sees that the things her spouse does, which she uses to justify her wrath, are in fact behaviors she herself helped create. She may realize that her perceptions of the situation were colored by her own anxiety. In other words, she begins to see she actually played a *role* in her spouse's behavior. Psychiatrist Michael Kerr helpfully describes the key to progress in a marriage this way:

There are two particularly important elements that influence the success of therapy for conflictual marriages:

1. people's ability to recognize the effect of anxiety and emotional reactivity on their own and on their spouse's behavior, and

2. people's ability to see that many of the things they use to justify the rejection and condemnation of the spouse are things they themselves help create.[10]

Many of us become experts on how our spouse unfairly blames us. Even if our perspective happens to be objectively true, it's a dead-end because it's hard to change other people. We may find it much more empowering to focus on the things over which we have control, namely, our own role in the blaming that takes place in our marriages. Remember the Serenity Prayer from twelve-step programs? "God, grant me the serenity to accept the things I cannot change, the courage to change the things I can, and the wisdom to know the difference." What we're discussing here is new wisdom to help us discern the difference between objective reality and anxious blame.

Many of us spend most of our lives stuck in Blaming Our Spouse because of the control our anxiety has over us. Aside from the occasional enlightened Master, it's been like that for millennia. Sadly, we don't realize we're in fight-or-flight mode until it's too late for our marriages. But take heart. Whether you're on your first marriage or your third, to recognize that anxiety is a factor in your criticism of your spouse is the first necessary step in order to pull out of the downward spiral of Blaming Your Spouse.

Because our fight-or-flight instinct so dominates our brains, we're not to blame (so to speak) for our less-than-resourceful blaming behavior. However, we need to become aware of our instincts so we can stop Blaming Our Spouse and avoid harming our marriage. The first step is becoming aware of how we delude ourselves that our criticism of our spouse is always accurate. Here's an example of what that first step of progress might look like.

Alan and his wife, Debbie, are driving to his mother's house for a visit. Alan notices that Debbie seems to be doing a lot of annoying things and making mistakes. He thinks his criticism of Debbie is justified, but in fact, he's acting out of the anxiety that's building within him as he anticipates being in the same room with his mom (Alan and his mom don't get along very well). Alan's anxiety has heightened his irritability, so little things Debbie does seem like a big deal to him. Debbie's behavior, in fact, hasn't changed.

But Alan catches himself snapping at Debbie, and realizes, "Hey — I'm focusing a lot on Debbie's behavior. Whenever I'm finding fault with others, that's usually a red flag that I'm anxious about something. I wonder what that could be. . . . "

We'll return to Alan and Debbie in chapter 7, but the message here is simply that, in a tense moment with our spouses, our anxious irritability may cloud our perceptions of our spouse.

If we could slow down the conversation in Debbie's brain about this incident with Alan, it would go something like this: "Do I argue with Alan on this point (fight response), or say nothing because he'll never listen anyway (flight response)?" The blame we feel in this tense situation is the same, but sometimes we respond by fighting and other times we choose flight. We may not physically run away, but we may emotionally distance ourselves.

Our flight mode is harder to spot than our fight mode. But fear of conflict or fear of the unknown may cause us to avoid unpleasant issues. The less a couple is talking, the more they eventually drift apart. That's why fear can be even more costly than anger, if it causes the slow, insidious erosion of our relationships.

As I mentioned above, Distancing from Our Spouse is the *flight* part of the fight-or-flight response. We look at distancing in the next chapter, and learn more about why arguing may be the least of all evils in dealing with anxiety in a family.

# Chapter Four

# The Silent Killer of Marriage

When the kids rushed off to play outside after dinner, James and Hannah would often linger at the dinner table, leisurely enjoying each other's company and discussing how their day had gone. One evening, Hannah brought up a problem she was having with her colleague at work. James thought the solution was obvious and suggested she stand up to this colleague. Hannah felt annoyed that James would rush to offer advice without understanding all the nuances of her work context. That pushed her buttons, so as a result, she suddenly called the kids in to help them with their homework. The moment of kitchen table intimacy was broken.

On another evening after dinner, Hannah was resting her feet on James's chair as James told her how much he had enjoyed riding in his buddy's new sports car that day. He and Hannah reminisced about his old Mustang they had driven around campus when they were dating in college. James mentioned how tax season was approaching and maybe their tax refund check could be a down-payment on a fun, new car. Hearing the word "taxes" really jarred Hannah, because money and taxes stress her out, especially that time of year. She abruptly got up and went into the kitchen to stack the dishwasher. James sensed he had said something to push her buttons, but wasn't sure what it was.

During their postdinner conversation only a few days later, Hannah brought up the possibility of changing their usual holiday routine that year. Instead of spending Thanksgiving with her family, and Christmas with James's family, she wanted to do the reverse. This was a touchy topic because James's family was very religious, and relatives came from near and far to celebrate this Christian holy day. Hannah began to explain her feelings on the matter, but James concluded to himself that she'd never listen to his side anyway, so he left the table. "Where are you going?" Hannah asked. "To the bathroom," James said. Hannah waited for him at the table, but he went upstairs and didn't come down again.

This was a typical pattern in the family of Hannah and James. While it may be tempting to take sides and pick which spouse you think was in the right in the examples above, the point here is not who's right and who's wrong. The important thing to notice is the pattern that emerges. On some evenings, Hannah decided that the kids' homework *must* begin at a particular moment and on another evening, she suddenly *had* to do the dishes instead of continue to talk. Likewise, James was *dying* to go to the bathroom and did not return.

All of Hannah's and James's activities are of course reasonable in and of themselves, but the *timing* is critical to our purposes. Hannah stood up from the dinner table at the moment her buttons were pushed, and James did likewise. The subtle message was, "If you *go there,* I'll leave." So even without realizing it, over time they began to avoid certain topics, so as not to lose their spouse's company at the table. . . .

We have already looked at two of the three main ways couples deal with tension in their marriages: Projection onto

Our Children, and Blaming Our Spouse. The third way is Distancing from Our Spouse. It is a silent killer of marriage, as well as the cause of many problems in our children.

In the name of keeping the peace, we are starving our marriages of emotional engagement and intimacy. We need to understand that it's much better to argue occasionally than to slowly go numb from avoiding each other. And it's much better to laugh, have fun, and make love in a marriage than to do more tasks for the children and the house.

What makes distancing so dangerous is that we may be completely blind to it. We may have some awareness of our fight response when we get really angry. But most of us have no awareness whatsoever of our *flight* response. It's such an automatic behavior that you almost don't have a choice in your actions. Your button gets pushed, suddenly some task becomes "urgent," and you're *outta there*. After all, the tasks we do when we Distance from Our Spouse seem much more noble and essential than an unpleasant argument.

Distancing is insidious because it creeps up so slowly that we don't notice it. Ten days or ten months of distancing means a lot of stuff gets done around the house. But ten *years* of distancing could mean our sex life has dwindled, and we feel more numbness than affection toward our spouse.

When couples come to me for coaching, they describe various problems that they believe are the cause of their marital discord. In my experience, many of their problems are merely symptoms of a distancing pattern that lurks beneath their marriage. They have no problem analyzing their arguments for hours. But when I ask them how they distance from each other, I'm often met with silence and a blank stare. We are not aware of how we may be starving our marriages to death.

This chapter answers the question, "Why do some couples seldom argue but still end up divorced, or with a troubled child?" We will cover five essential points:

1. Distancing is the *flight* element of our fight-or-flight response.

2. Distancing *seems* peaceful, but ultimately it's more destructive than arguing.

3. Common ways we distance include: the Silent Treatment, Cell Phones/Laptops/TV, Projection onto Our Children, and *Emotional Divorce*.

4. Emotional Divorce may mean moving *away from* our spouse, but *closer to* our child; this is a big problem.

5. Awareness of distancing is the key, because we can't change what we can't see.

This information is crucial because avoiding your spouse, over time, creates an unhappy marriage. As you move away from your spouse, you're also more likely to move toward your children, and overparenting causes more family problems.

## The "Flight" in Our Fight-or-Flight Response

Today's couples are quick to squelch the urge to argue with each other. But just because you rarely argue doesn't mean your marriage is strong.

Humans have forgotten we are animals. We may be the most intelligent animals, but our fight-or-flight response often hijacks our brains many times each day. It's easy to recognize our fight mode when we snap at our spouse or honk at the jerk on the freeway. However, we don't realize we may be in *flight* mode from our spouses when we switch on the TV, pour that extra drink, or shuttle the kids to yet another lesson.

Our two favorite avoidance behaviors are: (1) more time at work, and (2) more time with the kids. These behaviors may seem harmless, and even valuable, but they can be a slippery slope, leading to a distant marriage and Projection onto Our Children.

So the bad news is that distancing plays more of a role than we realize in the development of a marital problem. The good news is that we are innocently ignorant of how we distance, and once we begin to understand our role, we can roll up our sleeves and get to work on it. It's never too late to build a dependable friendship with our spouse that can last a lifetime.

The dinner-table examples of James and Hannah are typical of many American couples. They are busy. But Americans sometimes hide behind the façade of being busy. We do tasks to Distance from Our Spouses.

Productivity is of course a good thing. It's nice to have a clean house and well-tended children. It's important to answer that cell phone call so as not to lose a business opportunity. To be competitive in the workplace, we have to put in the time to stay on top of our e-mail and keep all the balls in the air with our projects.

But there's a difference between being busy and Distancing from Your Spouse. Sometimes being busy masks an underlying tension in the marriage. Intimate relationships are both the best and the hardest things we do, and sometimes being intimate is highly confrontational. We may feel vulnerable, or see something we don't like in our partner; or (most confrontional) see something we don't like about ourselves. Intimacy pushes our buttons.

What does it mean to have our buttons pushed? It usually happens in a split second, largely beneath our awareness. Our anxiety or irritability spikes, and without realizing it we kick into fight-or-flight mode. But fighting is unpleasant, so our brain may opt for flight mode, where we can use a task as an excuse to leave the conversation. Fighting is overt, but flight can be easily justified: after all, the dishes do need to be done, and the kids do need help with their homework, right?

Here is a place where many of us delude ourselves: flight may seem more pleasant than fighting, but its effects add up, as we see in the following example.

## Avoiding Our Spouse Is Worse Than Arguing

Chris was stunned when his wife of twelve years asked for a divorce. They seldom fought, and he thought everything was fine.

At first he was full of anger and blame, but looking back on their years together, Chris began to notice a pattern. He noticed that his wife had certain habits that really annoyed or even distressed him. However, he knew that if he brought these things up to his wife, they would argue and things would escalate.

So he just retreated into himself rather than trying to talk things out. He had always thought it was noble to keep the peace.

In retrospect, however, Chris could see that each time he retreated into himself, he moved one more millimeter away from his spouse, and they grew one degree colder toward each other. Over the years, those millimeters and degrees added up, until the couple became distant and chilly. This was one of those divorces where their family and friends were shocked, saying, "How could this be? They never fought, and everything seemed fine...."

Distancing is a silent killer because each time we avoid our spouse, it's a move away from him or her. It's hard to notice how far a couple has grown apart until some crisis forces them out of their chronic denial of the dilapidated state of their relationship.

Distancing is incredibly harmful, exactly *because* it appears so beneficial. Fighting is unpleasant, and distancing from each other in order to keep the peace seems mature. But the goal in marriage must not be to argue less. The emotional engagement of arguing — unpleasant as it can be — offers some catharsis, so it's much better in the long run than a slow distancing from your spouse.

Contrary to popular belief, there's absolutely nothing neutral about avoidance. The flight response stems from the same anxious panic in our brain as the fight response. We avoid difficult people and touchy topics because we're afraid: afraid of our anger, afraid of our vulnerability, or afraid of confrontation and escalation. That desire to run away, whether physically or emotionally, is anything but neutral. It is an anxious, knee-jerk reaction that harkens back to our cave man days.

Now, of course, sometimes avoiding or postponing a discussion is the best way to reach a thoughtful decision.

Given the choice between an argument and restraining ourselves from saying what we really think, who wouldn't
choose the path of peace? But I'm talking about the dozens
of knee-jerk flight responses with our spouse that slowly
become hundreds, and then thousands of avoidances. All
those little squelches quietly and insidiously accumulate
until the sum of those squelches becomes far greater than
a couple of explosive arguments would have been. With
arguments, at least there's some sense of purging one's feelings. With accumulated squelches, there's just bitterness and
resentment.

Our flight response stays under our radar, so it's the animal
instinct we most need to work hard to acknowledge. Our
first task is to learn to spot distancing in our marriage. The
more we can raise consciousness of our knee-jerk avoidance
behaviors, the more intimacy we can build with our spouses.
And if we don't distance as much from our spouses, our kids
will be less vulnerable to being projected upon by one spouse
who has fled the other spouse.

## Common Ways We Distance
## without Realizing It

Distancing is so subtle it often hides right under our
noses. Here are several common patterns we so often fail to
recognize in the moment.

### The Silent Treatment

A classic example of distancing is the Silent Treatment. It
is often wielded as a weapon in marriages, but is seldom
discussed outside the home. The Silent Treatment is a flight

response, in that it cuts off communication and promotes avoidance of one's spouse. But it also demonstrates the anger of the fight response, because it punishes the spouse passive-aggressively by withholding intimacy and approval. Few things shout anger more loudly than a tense silence. Stone-walling is an extreme example of the Silent Treatment, where a spouse's face goes blank, he falls angrily silent, and he leaves the room. Studies show that in 85 percent of cases of the Silent Treatment, men stonewall women, and the effects on their relationship can be devastating, because the silence makes any kind of discussion or resolution impossible.[1]

## Cell Phones and Laptops

Cell phones, portable wireless devices, and laptops are valuable tools that help us to get more things done more quickly. But sometimes we also (unconsciously) hide behind these tools to distance from our spouse.[2] They can be used to avoid interacting with a spouse. We should think about our motives when we answer a call or check our e-mail: Is it truly necessary, or just a well-justified distancing move?

## The Kids' Activities

Shuttling our kids to lessons, sports, and play-dates is a noble activity, with the best of intentions. But the way we go about it can be quite scattered and disconnected. Some kids describe their active parents as being "everywhere, and yet nowhere at the same time." We seem perpetually late, perpetually frazzled, and always focused on the next step of our busy day's schedule. Is shuttling moving us away from our spouses?[3]

## Distancing from Our Own Parents

If you're distancing from your parents, you're probably also distancing from your spouse.

Many of us mistakenly believe that distancing from our parents is evidence of our emotional independence. Our parents may have made choices we disagreed with or worse caused us harm — whether emotional or physical. Maybe distancing was necessary for a period, but our determination to be different from our parents may simply be our flight response in disguise. And it may backfire.

Just like avoiding hot-button topics with our spouse, distancing from our parents may appear peaceful, but that's only on the surface. Our flight response is just as much an anxious reaction as our fight response. In other words, distancing from one's parents is a clear indicator of the same emotional intensity as if one constantly argued with one's parents. The reality is that people who avoid their parents are still so emotionally enmeshed with them that being around their parents drives them crazy. Avoiding one's parents can mean visiting rarely or visiting often but avoiding personal or touchy topics — only discussing the weather, for example.

Here's the problem: Avoiding our parents is a sure sign of high anxiety and reactivity to our parents, which indicates Incomplete Weaning (discussed in chapter 2). This high anxiety probably affects how we relate to our spouses in our marriages as well.[4] In my observation, couples who distance in marriage often have a distant relationship with one or both of their parents. If we haven't handled our baggage with our parents, we've probably dragged it into our marriage. In other words, if our anxiety is driving our behavior, we tend to see only two options: either to change our parents' behavior or to withdraw. We may bring the same tendencies to our marriage as well.

But, besides changing our parents or withdrawing, there is a third option. We can train ourselves to rise above blame and distancing, while remaining part of our family. We will discuss this in chapter 7. It involves learning to notice our role in conflict, and the ways we may actually be creating the very problems we use to justify our blame of, or distancing from, our parents.[5]

### Emotional Divorce: Away from Our Spouse and toward our Child

Divorce is an extreme example of Distancing from Our Spouse. Like the Silent Treatment, divorce is often used as a fearful escape from the pain one feels toward a former lover, as well as a form of angry punishment against one's spouse.

But aside from legal divorce, there are many subtle ways that we commit emotional divorce from spouses every day. We avoid emotional topics that make us uncomfortable. We avoid making important decisions because we know that discussing them is likely to end in an argument. We avoid sharing our thoughts, feelings, or dreams with our spouse, because it may make us vulnerable to attack or ridicule.

But here is the danger of Emotional Divorce, and it's arguably the most important thing you'll read in this book: when we move away from our spouse in an Emotional Divorce, we never remain alone. We often move toward our children by becoming too attached, anxiously overfocusing on a child's defect, or both.

In today's society, Projection onto Our Children has become so common that few of us even recognize it as a problem. In fact, as I presented in chapter 1, most of us believe making our children the center of our lives is a normal, child-friendly thing to do.

It may be common, but it is not healthy.

Psychiatrist Michael Kerr describes the dynamics between the couples he counsels and their children. A child picks up on his two parents' marital discord via his attunement with one or both parents. The child senses something wrong and he feels anxious, but he is not sure why. The anxiety he absorbs eventually hits critical mass, and he develops a symptom. This makes him have a "problem," which diverts the parents' anxiety away from each other and onto their child. Kerr writes:

> Through years of "training," such a person has learned to gravitate to the disharmony he senses in others, regardless of whether an "invitation" is actually extended. A poorly differentiated child often occupies this type of position with his parents. He predictably makes himself a problem whenever tension reaches a certain level between his parents. This draws one or both parents' focus to him, thus reducing the tension between them.[6]

If we think of every marriage as being on a continuum, some have more discord than others. On one end, you've got the couples with very little discord, so their child may not make himself a problem at all; or if he does, maybe it's something relatively minor, such as talking back to his teacher at school. At the other extreme, a couple may have tremendous marital discord, which they address by either fighting

openly or else distancing and driving their anxiety under-
ground. The child who gravitates in between his parents may
develop a much larger symptom, to soak up a lot more of the
tension between his parents. He becomes a kind of willing,
yet unconscious scapegoat: he acts without thinking, and
he doesn't realize the consequences for his own health or
behavior.

Here's an extreme but eye-opening example. You may recall
that in chapter 1 I mentioned psychiatrist Murray Bowen's
observation of the parents of schizophrenics at the National
Institute of Mental Health. He described how there is

> a striking emotional distance between the parents in
> all the families with a schizophrenic child. We have
> called this the "emotional divorce." ... It was difficult
> for them to share personal feelings, thoughts, and expe-
> riences. But they avoided the touchy points to keep
> arguments at a minimum. They saw their marriages as
> difficult situations to be endured.[7]

Of course, these parents would not say their children
became schizophrenics because the parents moved away from
each other and moved toward the child by overfocusing on
the child's small defects. The parents would say the child
exhibited worrisome symptoms, which forced the parents to
pay attention and take action.

One may debate whether the parents' distant marriage
*caused* their children's schizophrenia, but Bowen's research
confirms that the couple's distance at least *contributed* to it.
In all ten families he studied at length, Bowen saw the same
pattern where one child became the scapegoat for the family's high anxiety. He also noted that in all ten cases, both

parents and patients unknowingly played a role in making this happen.[8]

As we saw in Michael Kerr's research, a child's attunement with and sensitivity to his parents appears to train him to get into the middle of his parents' tension. Once the child's sensitive nervous system absorbs anxiety to the point of overload, he develops a symptom.

It seems perfectly natural in this chicken-or-the-egg scenario for the parents to assume their child's symptoms preceded their worry. Projection takes place beneath our awareness, and, as we asked in chapter 1, what parent is willing to confront the fact that her child might be suffering symptoms because of her behavior?

There is some comfort in knowing that it's not one parent's fault. Rather, one parent begins to project *only because* both parents are distancing from each other.

That's the hidden cost of Emotional Divorce: when we move away from our spouse, we may move toward our child. And *neither* parent is to blame, because their distancing takes place beneath their awareness.

No one is responsible, because they didn't realize what they were doing. But they can improve their family by first becoming aware of the distancing in their marriage, and then noticing the Projection onto Their Child.

◆ ◆ ◆

We have now learned the three behaviors that couples use to deal with marital tension: Projection onto Our Children, Blaming Our Spouse, and Distancing from Our Spouse. This of course raises the question, What causes us to resort to such behaviors when they clearly don't serve our goals of raising happy kids and staying happily married?

The answer is anxiety, the root of all our negative behaviors. I have alluded to anxiety throughout the first chapters, and now we will examine it in more detail.

# Chapter Five

# Anxiety:
# The Cause of Drama
# in Relationships

Andy had an affair. His wife, Jill, was devastated. All Jill's family and friends told her Andy was a jerk to betray her like that. Society condemns Andy. He seems to be the bad guy, and Jill seems to be the hapless victim.

But beneath this sad situation lies a typical pattern of behavior that can lead to an extramarital affair:

Soon after they married, Jill and Andy were surprised at the levels of tension, conflict, or dissatisfaction they felt for each other. At first, they tried to communicate their feelings of hurt and talk it out in order to resolve their differences. Over time, this didn't seem to be working, so they'd lose patience and argue more often. But open conflict is unpleasant for everyone, and society has taught them that arguing and anger are bad things that doom a marriage.

So whether consciously or not, they decided to keep the peace, and avoid the touchy topics. They communicated less of their true thoughts, feelings, and dreams to each other. They distanced from each other, and turned to other passions. He married his career, and she married the kids. Everything seemed fine: they seldom argued, he was succeeding at his career, and she was meeting her intimacy needs with the children.

But over the years, their distancing gradually became a problem. Andy's job obviously couldn't meet his intimacy needs, so in a moment of temptation he started having an affair.

I am not condoning extramarital affairs. What Andy did was wrong. But his affair was only a symptom of the distancing pattern that had been going on for years. Unfortunately, however, by the time a couple seeks help, all they focus on is The Problem, saying what a jerk Andy is. They believe his selfishness is the cause of the affair.

But The Problem is actually just one symptom of Andy and Jill's anxiety. Their anxiety had been triggering their fight-or-flight response for years, so they alternated between blame and avoidance, which eventually brought down their marriage. The affair was the proverbial straw that broke the camel's back.

I'm not saying what Andy did was right and what Jill did was wrong. I'm saying it was almost inevitable. It takes two to tango, but neither spouse has any awareness that their inner anxiety had made them trigger-happy — predisposed to blaming and distancing.

This chapter answers the question: Why do humans have so much drama in our families?

This chapter will cover six points:

1. What we call stress is actually our inner anxiety.

2. Anxiety is a primal survival instinct that protected us well back in our cave man days; now it makes us treat our relationships as if "it's a jungle out there."

3. Anxiety is what makes people irritable and quick to overreact.

4. The two main causes of anxiety are Incomplete Weaning (as we saw in chapter 2) and *Imprinting*.

5. *Imprinting* means that as children, we soaked up our family's drama by attunement, and that's where we get our buttons that are easily pushed in relationships.

6. Knowledge is power. We'll review examples of how anxiety causes the drama in our families (i.e., projection, blame, and distancing).

These points are crucial because you'll learn what causes us to become irritable and overreactive — namely, anxiety. Once we understand how anxiety works within ourselves, we can transform our knee-jerk reactions into thoughtful responses and reduce the drama in our families.

## What We Call "Stress" Is Actually Our Own Inner Anxiety

We often confuse the concepts of stress and anxiety. Most of us think of stress as an external force in our lives, and it is. However, when we say we're stressed, we're usually referring to that uncomfortable feeling of tension within. That inner tension is more accurately called *anxiety*.

In chapter 2 we discussed in detail how we soak up anxiety by osmosis through our attunement with our primary caregivers. The less completely we are weaned as children, the more we are programmed for anxiety in our adult relationships.

Whereas our relationship with our primary caregiver is a source of anxiety, humans also have anxiety as a primal instinct that's been with us as long as animals have been eating each other. In our cave man days, anxiety helped us to anticipate danger, so it was a valuable survival instinct that kept us on guard against threats. But today we don't think of it as such. We think of anxiety as a bad, uneasy feeling that we want to get rid of as quickly as possible.

In prehistoric times, humans didn't start out as the dominant species. We were prey. Evolutionary biologists believe anxiety is an ancient instinct, etched into our brains during a time when how fast we reacted to threats could mean the difference between life or death. Anxiety helped us to anticipate danger and decide if we wanted to fight back or run away. Anxiety mobilized us to protect our families from danger so that we could safely raise offspring. Through survival of the fittest, our ancestors passed on this genetic advantage, and here we are today, equipped with an overdeveloped sense of anxiety in an environment devoid of many of the natural threats that warranted heightened anxiety in the first place.[1]

Our guardian instinct of anxiety was nature's brilliant evolutionary solution to survival: it enabled us to scan the environment for predators or enemies, always trying to anticipate potential threats before they happened. You might say that predators or enemies were "stressors," and so we needed plenty of anxiety to anticipate our enemies and be vigilant against predators. In response, our brains evolved a complex circuitry of neurons and hormones that today are known as the stress response, which triggers fight or flight.

The stress response begins in the lower part of the brain with a small, almond-shaped mass of neurons called the amygdala. In chapter 2, we touched upon the role of the amygdala in storing different memories in an effort to avoid a repeat of difficult situations we had already encountered. Now we will examine in more depth the amygdala and its key role in producing the anxiety we feel.

## A Nervous Soldier on Guard Duty

A useful metaphor is to think of the amygdala as a nervous soldier on guard duty, ever vigilant and ready to protect us from danger by setting off our fight-or-flight response.

If the amygdala perceives a threat, it trips the alarm to produce adrenaline and cortisol. These messenger hormones shoot through the body, diverting blood to our muscles and readying us for fight or flight. As Daniel Goleman notes, "The amygdala's extensive web of neural connections allows it, during an emotional emergency, to capture and drive much of the rest of the brain — including the rational mind."[2]

To take our metaphor of a soldier on guard duty a step further: A calm soldier can focus objectively on the genuine movements and noises in the bushes. Unfortunately, the "nervous soldier" that is our amygdala sometimes overreacts to shadows or the slightest rustling noise he hears in the bush. That nervous soldier may be filled with all kinds of insecurities and stories he's heard that make him jumpy. This greatly increases the likelihood that he'll overreact and trip the alarm even when it's not necessary. The nervous soldier can be trigger-happy.

Likewise with the human mind. We rely on our guardian instinct to make snap decisions about whether we're truly threatened or not. In order to make these split-second decisions, the amygdala doesn't just respond thoughtfully and carefully to outside stressors in the moment. As we saw in chapter 2, the amygdala is the Keeper of the Scary Memories, so it quickly compares the situation at hand with its memories of similar situations in the past.

When our brain's stress response jumps to action, one of the first things it does is commandeer the part of the brain responsible for logic and reason, the prefrontal cortex. Suddenly, our brain's headquarters for thoughtful responses has been hijacked by the amygdala's knee-jerk reactions. Its snap judgments are unfortunately based on scanty evidence that then gets compared with memories of overreactions of the past — not the most desirable strategy we'd like for our interactions with others.[3]

This means that if one's amygdala is hypervigilant and prone to overreact, it's hard for that person to think clearly. In the name of speed, the amygdala just makes a quick-and-dirty assessment, so overreactions are common. A person with an overreactive amygdala will often end up in fight-or-flight mode when a thoughtful, compassionate response might have served her better.

## Is It a Jungle Out There?

The problem is that our brains have not evolved as quickly as our society. Back when our ancestors faced life-and-death decisions on a daily basis, anxiety was a highly useful survival mechanism, which dictated a large portion of our behavior. The choices were blunt: eat or be eaten. A decisive, quick-and-dirty appraisal by our amygdalas was all we needed to act. If, for example, we overreacted and fled from a perceived threat that turned out to be nothing, no great harm done — we just got some extra exercise that day.

When humans lived in the wilderness, it was good to have a trigger-happy amygdala. This stress-response served us well for the last fifty thousand generations, but the problem is that modern society has evolved much more quickly than our brains have evolved. Today, our amygdala's constant overreactions to perceived insults get us into trouble more often than they get us out of trouble.

Today if we overreact and flee unnecessarily, there may be great harm done to our relationships. Modern relationships are much more complex than friend-or-foe, eat or be eaten. We can't walk into the boardroom with a cave man's club, or sit at our family dinner table, poised to pounce or flee. Negotiating all the gray areas of relationships requires much more subtlety and nuance than our outdated amygdalas offer.[4] In a sense, we're trying to do our job in life with outdated equipment.

Our collective amygdalas have gone into overdrive in the past century, even though our lives actually have become much safer in the developed world. Miracle drugs like penicillin have effectively combatted infection and plagues. Better nutrition has greatly decreased the odds we might die young. We now live 60 percent longer than we did only a hundred years ago. Yet, even as the actual daily threats to life and limb are *dramatically* lower than ever, we've been overreacting to everything lately: from road rage and helicopter parenting to insomnia, depression, and excessive medication use. Therefore, it should be no surprise that we're overreacting to our spouses more and getting divorced at an alarming rate.[5] What, exactly, is going on in our heads?

We humans take great pride in our cerebral superiority over our animal cousins. We can all pat ourselves on the back that the human brain has tripled in volume over just the last 2.5 million years,[6] an astonishing rate of growth. Yes, we have a marvelous prefrontal cortex that gives us the logic and speech that our animal cousins don't enjoy.

But when we're in the clutch, we shouldn't be so proud. In moments of anger or fear, we're just as *animal* as any other animal. Why? Because our fight-or-flight instinct still rules the roost in our big, fat brains. Size doesn't matter (much). To oversimplify, our brain has three parts: The oldest, most instinctive part of our brain is the reptile brain. It is located at the base of the skull and is home to the fight-or-flight instinct. The reptile brain did an admirable job of helping us survive back in an era when there were no police or court systems: you either fought with enemies, or ran like hell. The other two parts of our brain, the limbic and the cortex, evolved much later, and piled on top of the reptile brain in our skulls. Thanks to these new additions to our brain we now enjoy speech, planning, organization, and civilized society.

The only problem is that when there's a crisis, the brain knows who's boss. No matter what reasonable, logical responses the cortex (the thinking portion) may be sending to our lips, our reptile brain (the instinctive portion) sits on the controls. Strategically positioned atop our spinal cords, the reptile brain controls the messages to our bodies. And the reptile brain's approach is, shall we say, a little less subtle than our cortex: attack or retreat. It chooses and acts in a nanosecond.

As we will discuss later in this chapter, the ideal is for us to bring the fight-or-flight process into our conscious minds in order for the thinking part of our brains to take more control. Unfortunately, these days our thinking cortex often ends up more as the spin doctor for our amygdala's brash ways, spinning impressive, intellectual justifications for why we have done the dumb things we do.[7]

It's too bad we don't behave more often according to our cortex. Whereas the thoughtful cortex can see and process complex information in shades of gray, the amygdala and reptile brain specialize in snap judgments: they perceive everything in black-and-white. If the amygdala perceives a threat, it acts first and thinks later. Daniel Goleman sums it up this way:

> Such imprecision in, say, a squirrel, is fine, since it leads to erring on the side of safety, springing away at the first sign of anything that might signal a looming enemy, or springing toward a hint of something edible. But in human emotional life that imprecision can have disastrous consequences for our relationships, since it means, figuratively speaking, we can spring at or away from the wrong thing — or person. . . . If the amygdala senses a sensory pattern of import emerging, it jumps to a conclusion, triggering its reactions before there is full confirming evidence — or any confirmation at all.
>
> Small wonder we can have so little insight into the murk of our more explosive emotions, especially while they still hold us in thrall. The amygdala can react

in a delirium of rage or fear before the cortex knows
what is going on because such raw emotion is triggered
independent of, and prior to, thought.[8]

In other words, it's hard for us to respond thoughtfully
when our amygdala is running the show.

## Programmed to Overreact

When we describe people as having a chip on their shoulder,
what we mean is that they are often so caught up in the thrall
of their explosive emotions that they perceive everything in
black and white. Their chip may seem obvious to us, but they
honestly don't see the role they play in creating the drama
and conflict in their lives. Their high levels of anxiety leave
them stuck in a loop of chronic overreaction. Their amygdala
overreacts to a perceived slight, it stores memories of what
triggered it, then later it overreacts when those memories are
triggered by similar touchy situations.

Over time, and with many stored memories, the amygdala
becomes sloppy at distinguishing a friendly overture from a
threat, and it errs on the side of perceiving threats (paranoia).
The amygdala further overpowers the thoughtful cortex and
hijacks the brain, creating a chronic state of high alert and
overreaction. That means the brain is perpetually trigger-
happy, assuming the worst of every comment or scenario.
The result? The owner of such a brain would be described
as having a chip on his shoulder.[9]

So how to break this vicious cycle and get the chip off
our own shoulder? The biggest challenge in self-awareness is
to realize that we often put the cart before the horse when

it comes to thinking versus feeling. We tend to believe our thoughts are rational most of the time, so we perceive our judgments and criticisms to be rational and justified. In fact, we're mostly reacting to irrational feelings based on the snap judgment of our anxious amygdala run amok. To make matters worse, our anxious brain often recruits our thinking brain after the fact to justify our knee-jerk reactions.[10]

When we're anxious, we may see things exactly backward. Our anxiety causes us to have "issues," rather than our issues causing us to have anxiety. That is to say, people with a chip on their shoulder believe they're perceiving the world objectively. They don't realize their overhyped amygdalas are often running the show. As the science fiction writer Robert Heinlein noted, "Man is not a rational animal, but a rationalizing one."

The good news is that we can take back our brains from our overreactive amygdalas by bringing this mostly unconscious process into our conscious awareness. We need to be able to spot just how often it's our anxiety talking rather than our supposedly clear judgment. This awareness can be like seeing behind the curtain in *The Wizard of Oz*. We find anxiety driving the majority of our feelings and actions, as well as the feelings and actions of our loved ones.

How can we bring our unconscious anxiety into our conscious minds? We study the unspoken conversations in our families of origin that shaped our behavior. Remember chapter 2, which discussed attunement as the honest, candid messenger of what our parents were *really* worried about? Well, we have to do some detective work to find out just what our families were teaching us — not by their words, but by our attunement with them. The following section presents an example of what I mean.

## Imprinting: How We Pass Our Baggage On to Our Kids

Ninety years ago, Susan's husband went off to fight in World War I. He was listed as missing in action, and he never returned home. Two years after the war ended, Susan's neighbors saw her husband in a nearby city, very much alive, with another woman. Susan was devastated that her husband betrayed her and left her alone to raise their three daughters. Not surprisingly, Susan's daughters learned via their attunement with their mother to be distrustful of men. Susan was worried that the same thing could happen to her beloved children. Maybe she sat the girls down and had a frank discussion about it. More likely, her attunement with her daughters was the medium by which Susan's mind sent out danger signals regarding men, signals that her daughters picked up on unconsciously.

Over the years, however, Susan's bitterness and worry about her daughters' relationships became a self-fulfilling prophecy that sowed distrust of men in her daughters' minds. This anxiety was further exacerbated by the herd instinct among these three daughters, where one negative encounter with one boyfriend would increase the doubt and worry of the other two sisters. So the family's imprinting about men was spread contagiously among all three sisters and their mother, affecting their subsequent marriages. Even Susan's granddaughter Bridget was unconsciously mistrustful of men, although she didn't know exactly why, having never heard her grandma's ugly secret. Nonetheless, Bridget's ancestors' anxiety regarding men had pervaded Bridget's being, via her attunement with the loved ones in her household.

Unfortunately, Bridget's husband often worked late and seemed too chummy with his female colleague. Although he had no sexual intentions toward his colleague, Bridget began to anxiously overreact to her husband's working late. She created a self-fulfilling prophecy in which her unfounded suspicion of her husband's misdeeds drove them apart.

Susan's family is an example of the subtle, instinctive, and unfortunate manner by which we pass our baggage on to our kids. Here are the two concepts that are key to understanding this process, and we will examine both ideas in more detail below:

1. A child is growing up in an anxious household, where parents and siblings aren't aware of their anxiety that fuels their conflict, distancing, and projection.

2. The child's attunement allows her to pick up the anxious vibes of parents and siblings in the household, and her brain's *mirror neurons* allow the child to feel her family's anxiety within herself.

## Anxiety Spreads Quickly through the "Herd"

Humans are herd animals, and this fact has a much greater impact on our development than we realize. Zoologists place humans among the obligatorily gregarious species, because evolution has instilled a fear of ostracism that makes us social to the core. We feel a tremendous drive to fit in, to win approval, and to not make waves in a group. The discomfort we feel when family members dislike us, criticize us, or gossip about us is evidence of our social nature and our desire for togetherness.

Neuroscientists assert that the interaction of every sibling, grandparent, and cousin is a major factor influencing the brain development of our children. As we grow up in our families, we are constantly learning how to behave: by example, by teaching, and most importantly by attunement. Attunement allows us to assimilate the powerful messages our parents and siblings convey about what we should think about ourselves and others. Our family members' subtle verbal and nonverbal cues create neuronal pathways in our fledgling brains. These neuronal pathways become our habitual ways of thinking and reacting to people around us, but we don't even understand where we acquired these habits that are so hard to break. Bridget's mind-set regarding men is an example of this unspoken training we receive in our families.

This process of learning about relationships through the osmosis of attunement is known as *imprinting*.

Imprinting is a fancy word for how our families "train" their offspring to behave through relationships. For example, in the Kalahari Desert of Africa, if a group of meerkats picks on a rogue member and shuns her, that meerkat is conditioned to conform, and the others learn from the example that was made of her. If she makes waves, she risks further retaliation. Likewise in human families, family members instinctively know the hundreds of unwritten rules that dictate their behavior within that family.

For example, if you imagine a fictitious family, perhaps your sister Jill is the big sister who dominates any conversation and usually gets her way. Jack may be the peacemaker who always tries to heal any conflicts in the family. Jane is the victim, who gets teased and fretted over by her siblings and seems sickly and weak. Dick is the black sheep, who always seems to get the blame even when he has done nothing wrong. Everyone seems to know the unwritten rules about who can do what to whom.

Often these rules become so entrenched that people take them for granted as inborn and unchangeable. Family members probably believe that the family unit didn't shape each member's behavior. Instead, they believe that their individual behavior is caused by innate, inborn personality traits, since each member of the family "has always been like that."

In fact, a child growing up in a family environment soaks up the family dynamics like a sponge. Learning by osmosis begins with the strong attunement she has with her mother and father. Kids pick up on everything, so she takes in the way her parents and siblings handle their own emotional storms, and then she apes that behavior herself.[11]

Attunement is helpful because it lays down neuronal pathways in our brain that allow us to learn from the example of our parents about navigating the challenges of life. The problem is that sometimes imprinted behavior is more hurtful than helpful, such as when unhealthy behavior is imprinted and passed down through generations. We saw this with our earlier example of Susan and her granddaughter Bridget. These pathways become "ruts," or automatic knee-jerk reactions, that often do not serve us well. Our ancestors may pass on their fears in the form of our family's "groupthink," which we absorb by attunement, often without question or even awareness.

This negative imprinting determines many of our "buttons" that can get pushed easily, and imprinting also determines what kind of role we play in our family of origin — the same role we unconsciously tend to play in all our relationships. One could say that our role, and many of our behaviors, were programmed into us by the imprinting of our family of origin.

We have now examined the three main ways we pass our baggage on to our kids: Imprinting, Incomplete Weaning (discussed in chapter 2), and Projection onto Our Children (discussed in chapter 1). Unless a family becomes aware of the process, their baggage continues to be handed down through the generations, and attunement is the main medium of communication.

## Incomplete Weaning versus Imprinting

How do Incomplete Weaning and Imprinting compare?

First, let's look at their important similarities. The degree of weaning or imprinting a child receives comes mostly from her parents. The way the child's Weaning or Imprinting is communicated is mainly through unspoken attunement with family members. It is the mirror neurons, in the brain of the child, that soak up the feelings from attunement and re-create those same feelings within the child's brain. Rather than "monkey see, monkey do," it's more like, "monkey feel, monkey duplicate same feelings within."

Now for the differences between Incomplete Weaning and Imprinting.

Incomplete Weaning stems from the balance of the mother-infant bond and the weaning instinct. Weaning is the degree to which we have separated from the mother-infant bond. The less we are weaned, the more anxiety we pick up via attunement, which creates more overreactive amygdala memories we store, which in turn contributes to higher reactivity in relationships.

On the other hand, Imprinting stems mostly from our herd instincts. Every household is a herd, and every interaction in that herd's web of relationships is soaked up by a child, and it influences the neuronal pathways being laid down in the child's developing mind. It is mainly the herd that determines what role a child will grow up to play in the family, and it is the herd that spreads anxiety like wildfire. There is plenty of emotional overlap between the herd-leaders, the parents, and siblings or relatives living under the same roof, and the herd tends to follow and amplify whatever vibe is passed down from the parent-leaders.

Our Imprinting comes from our families of origin — the role we develop as a member of a herd, where our interactions within this complex web of relationships shape us. Via attunement, we pick up on the anxiety and the subtle messages being passed around the herd at any given time, and this affects both the role we play and the anxiety we absorb from or spray onto others.

Usually, Imprinting is not as simple as passing one role down from generation to generation, such as, "Grandpa was an alcoholic, so his children and grandchildren became alcoholics." It's the *anxiety* passed down that causes a family member to take on a role, such as, "Grandpa was anxious, so his children and grandchildren also had high anxiety, which manifested in various symptoms." Here's a real-life example of family roles, taken from Ava's family, where her dad's Post-traumatic Stress Disorder (PTSD) led to some of his grandchildren's problems.

Ava's father, who had already been an anxious person, came back from World War II with PTSD, even though many of his comrades, who encountered the same battle conditions, did not develop PTSD. So his daughter, Ava, grew up in a highly anxious environment and was imprinted with her father's legacy of high anxiety and reactivity.

Because Ava was highly anxious herself, she tended to worry too much about her children, which became a self-fulfilling prophecy. She was unaware that she projected her anxiety onto her kids, and her family ended up with one child with depression, two children with severe asthma, and three children who got divorced. When Ava's children had children themselves, one was diagnosed with ADHD, another was diagnosed with depression, and almost all of them have had trouble maintaining a stable intimate relationship. The common denominator, passed on from generation to generation, was anxiety. We don't pass on the same symptoms; we pass on high levels of anxiety that then manifest as various symptoms. We can't help passing our anxiety onto our children unless we first become aware of the process.

## Kids Pick Up On Everything: Mirror Neurons

This section examines how a child's attunement picks up the anxious vibe of the household, and her brain's *mirror neurons* cause her to feel her family's anxiety within herself.

Anxiety is contagious, and mammalian offspring instinctively depend on their parents for survival, so if a kid's parent is anxious about something, the child innately senses that he or she ought to be anxious too. There's a reciprocity that feeds on itself and quickly escalates. It's not logical or conscious. We don't actively decide to take on someone else's anxiety. It's instinctive.

Anxiety spreads via the mirror neurons in our brains. Although many of us have never heard of mirror neurons, it may be helpful to learn of the large role they play in our daily lives.

Mirror neurons are responsible for making social animals sociable. To repeat an earlier metaphor, it's like "monkey see, monkey *feel*." When we feel another person's "vibes," it's our mirror neurons that imitate the feelings we perceive as emanating from that person. Our brain's internal imitation of a person's body language or feelings is what gives us a sense of empathy, or feeling in synch, or feeling chemistry, for another person. It is our mirror neurons that put us in synch with the feelings of others. That's what makes emotions so contagious among people, especially intimate loved ones.[12]

Mirror neurons evolved initially as a survival mechanism, because they helped spread anxiety in an instant — like the startle reflex of one gazelle that immediately spooks the whole herd into a stampede. The collective startle reflex of mirror neurons offered a tremendous advantage in keeping our ancestors safe. For example, as we see with gazelles, if one member of the herd was startled, much better for all to fly off than to stick around and see if there truly was a threat. This startle reflex is found among many animals, including humans. The distress of one instantly becomes the distress of all, in a kind of rapid-fire mirrored contagion.

So the species with this collective startle reflex survived because it gave them a safety advantage. Then they instinctively sought it out in the mates they selected, and the trait was further reinforced in their subsequent offspring. That's why panic spreads so quickly in animals, including humans.[13]

Mirror neurons are the likely path by which our primary caregiver programs us for anxiety. Our mirror neurons give us the empathy and sensitivity to pick up anxiety from our caregivers, via attunement. You might say attunement is the "monkey see" part of our previous expressions, "monkey see, monkey feel." And our mirror neurons are the "monkey feel" part. Attunement allows us to "see" much more of our caregivers' thoughts and feelings then they realize. Mirror neurons allow us to feel much more of the anxiety swirling around us than our parents realize, so we soak it up, even when we're too young to remember (as was the case with Bridget in my earlier example). This is how both imprinting and an overactive mother-infant bond can have such an impact on our psychological make-up as children.

Thus, the empathy that we associate with our intimate relationships had its primal origins in the mirror neurons of our brain. The anxious distress of our mate or our family was mirrored in our own brains, so that anxiety could instantly spread through a family and rouse us to action. Mirror neurons and attunement are the mechanisms by which anxiety is transmitted in a family.

In families where anxiety runs high, unfortunately, this means they are quick to blame, quick to distance, or quick to project. Generally speaking, families with higher anxiety have more arguments, more family members who don't speak to each other, and more problem behavior in their children.

To summarize Imprinting: Most families are not aware of their collective level of anxiety, or how contagious anxiety is among family members. Thus, parents and siblings aren't aware of how anxiety fuels their fighting, distancing, and projection onto children. But kids pick up on everything, through attunement, and they feel their family's anxiety in their own brains because of mirror neurons. Thus, the family members' unspoken, unconscious influence on the child's brain development imprints her character with the family viewpoint and habitual behaviors that become her "role" in her family, and ultimately in her relationships outside her family as well.

◆ ◆ ◆

All right, now we're going to use some real-life examples of the folks we've already heard about in previous chapters to illustrate how we pass our baggage on to our kids through Projection, Incomplete Weaning, and Imprinting.

## Seeing the Vicious Cycle of Anxiety

Let's consider the Big Picture. We have now examined all five aspects of the vicious circle that causes the drama in our families. We have discussed how Projection onto Our Children and Incomplete Weaning mess up our kids. We have identified how Blaming Our Spouse and Distancing from Our Spouse mess up our marriages, which in turn cause us to mess up our kids. And now we have just looked at how anxiety is at the root of all overreaction in relationships.

Anxiety causes us to blame and distance from our spouse. Blaming or Distancing from Our Spouse can cause us to project and overfocus on our kids. Projection and Incomplete Weaning program our kids to be anxious, which in turn primes them to blame and distance in their future marriages. In this manner, we pass our emotional baggage on to our kids, and so on onto future generations.

But, with an understanding of this vicious circle, we can stop the downward spiral for ourselves, our children, and their children.

As a review of what we have learned so far, let's go back to our real-life examples from each chapter. Let's see how the common denominator is always anxiety. For our review, I will give you a metaphor of "the boiling pots." This metaphor aims to show you how anxiety drives every step of the vicious circle that messes up our families.

Think of yourself as a four-quart pot on the stove. Anxiety is the boiling water within you, the four-quart pot.

It's not the most poetic of metaphors, but the image of you and your loved ones as pots of boiling water may bring you more clarity. Here's what I mean:

For example, let's say you are a woman of an average level of anxiety. Your pot is half full; say, two quarts of boiling water. You meet a guy who is also of average anxiety, that is to say, he has two quarts of boiling water in his pot. You feel chemistry for this guy and marry him, such that "the two shall become as one." Each of you poured your two quarts into the new pot that is your marriage — four quarts into one pot.

The problem is that your marriage pot is now full to the brim. Your marriage already has all the anxiety it can handle.

So when something comes along that causes you anxiety, it's pretty easy for your pot to boil over. Let's use this metaphor to look at our real-life examples.

Remember Bob and Jackie from chapter 3 on Blaming Your Spouse? Their pot was full too. So that night at the barbeque, Jackie was tired and irritable from the kids and close to a boil. Likewise, Bob was already at his boiling point from news of the letter that seemed to threaten his job security. Jackie gave Bob "that look," and they boiled over. Once they were boiling over and blaming each other, it was hard to get the lid back on that pot. They boiled over for the rest of that evening at home, because once their anxiety hit that boiling point where it triggered their fight response, it was hard to think clearly enough to turn down the temperature a few degrees and calm down.

Generally speaking, as our anxiety rises, we tend to be critical and blaming until we hit that boiling point, and then our fight response takes over our brain as we break into a full-blown argument.

Remember James and Hannah from chapter 4 on Distancing from Your Spouse? They enjoyed lingering at the table after meals, but their pot was also full to the brim with anxiety. Hannah was already near the boiling point when she came home from that tense interaction with her colleague at work. James picked up on the fact that Hannah was close to the boiling point, and that spiked his anxiety for two reasons: he cares about her, and anxiety is contagious: he feels uncomfortable being with her when she's upset.

So he anxiously tried to fix her to make everything calm down, but he had the opposite effect. Hannah already felt defensive because of her stress, so she heard James's advice as criticism, which caused her to hit the boiling point. The flight response kicked in, and she could no longer remain at the table. She had to flee, so suddenly she had to help the kids with their homework.

Next, let's go back to chapter 1 about Projecting onto Our Children, with Sabrina jumping to the conclusion that her son, Ian, must have allergies because he coughed a little in the night. Sabrina and her husband also had a full pot. The tension in their marriage and arguments about their finances turned up the heat and left both Sabrina and her husband near their boiling points. They had fought about this previously, but that morning her husband had a flight response and left for the office.

Again, anxiety is contagious, so his boiling brought Sabrina to a boil, which triggered her brain's defense mechanism of projection, such that when her son, Ian, coughed, she boiled over and the couple's anxiety spilled onto Ian in the form of projection. Once Ian had soaked up some of his parents' anxiety, their pot no longer overflowed so they felt better, but Ian was now "scalded" with a diagnosable health ailment.

In chapter 2, you may recall how Ann "married" her daughter, Nina, in order to give her all the love Ann felt her mother had withheld. When Nina was younger, everything seemed fine as both parties thrived on the mother-infant bond, but when Nina became a teenager, things changed. Nina now felt that her mother often let her down, so Nina's pot was almost constantly at the boiling point. The tension between Nina and her mom contributed to more misunderstandings and overreactions, which further lowered both of their boiling points. The chronic overreaction in this relationships also programs Nina to boil over easily in her future intimate relationships.

Finally, consider the story of Andy (who had an affair) and Jill earlier in this chapter. Andy and Jill each brought at least two quarts of hot, anxious water to their marriage, so right from the start it often came close to boiling. At first, they were able to turn down the temperature a bit by talking things through, but as their frustration and impatience grew, the pot of their marriage boiled over, first triggering their fight response and arguments.

Later, a sense of hopelessness and resignation set in, so they switched to flight response: Andy fled to his career, and Jill fled to the children. They probably thought their pot had stopped boiling, but remember: when we move away from our spouse, we always move toward something or someone. Andy eventually moved toward a "someone," and had an affair. Now we can see the consequences of denial: if they had been aware of the anxious, boiling pot of their marriage, they could have worked on their intimacy to make sure the pot didn't boil over into Andy having an affair or Jill projecting on their kids.

The point of these examples is for us to see how anxiety is at the root of the drama in our relationships.

## Relief from Anxiety: Self-Awareness

Now, here's the great news: knowledge is power. Anxiety is at its most powerful when we're not aware of it. So learning about our anxiety empowers us to deal with it more effectively. The simple act of reading this book may have already begun to improve your family life. Becoming aware that we blame and distance from our spouse or project onto our children may be difficult news to face. But awareness of how anxiety produces these patterns is our best preventive medicine to reduce the occurrence of these patterns and prevent the resultant problems from occurring in our families and being passed down through the generations.

Thinking trumps the fight-or-flight response in your brain. Each time you catch yourself blaming your loved one, hopefully now you'll wonder what you were anxious about that spiked your irritability. If you can recognize irritability as a marker of your anxiety, it helps you to stop the action and wonder if you're perceiving the situation as clearly as you thought. That shadow of a doubt, that sliver of uncertainty, is fantastic because it derails the autopilot of your instinctive reactions. The fight-or-flight response never wonders: it simply reacts in a split second. But if you're wondering, it means you're thinking. If you're thinking, it means you're not governed by your instincts alone. And the more you're thinking, the more willful control you have over your behavior. You've removed the tunnel-vision, black-and-white glasses and put on a more thoughtful response.

By raising our consciousness, we can reduce the blaming, distancing, and projecting in our families. By reading about this process, you have already partially disarmed it. Hopefully, you will never look at your family interactions the same way again. This new awareness may mean you'll pass on less of your baggage to your kids.

If you can begin to see the human family as a herd of animals who communicate by attunement, you'll be able to accept yourself more. You won't have to feel guilty about your mistakes because now you'll see how it was your anxiety that caused them, not that you're somehow a bad person. You can also change your behaviors more easily if you're less burdened by self-defeating thoughts. It's a relief to realize that the family you are born into largely determines how much anxiety you carry in your "pot" and how much you overreact. You can stop beating yourself up for the dumb things you do, but you must stop blaming others for your problems as well.

Now that you understand the source of your own problems, you realize that the same applies to all people. You know that what they're doing (as cruel or as dumb as it seems) is the best they can do, given the hand they were dealt in life. You can therefore become more tolerant of and compassionate toward others. You may spend less time trying to fix your loved ones, and more time trying to change yourself — which is where real empowerment lies.

And the news only gets better. The rest of this book is focused on solutions and practical tools you can use to reduce your anxiety, which reduces your blame, distancing, and projection. You've made it through the uncomfortable, confrontational part of this book.

I'm committed to helping you stay more happily married and raise happier kids. That's what this book is all about. Here are the practical tools I'm going to discuss in the following chapters.

In chapter 6, I'll explain how Mother Nature gave us chemistry to ensure we married the perfect mate for us. Once we realize the grass is not greener on the other side of the fence, we can settle down to create the best marriage possible.

In chapter 7, we'll go on safari in our families of origin to learn how we were programmed for anxiety as children and how we can reduce it as adults.

In chapter 8, we'll discuss how to fix problems in our children by fixing them in ourselves.

In chapter 9, we'll learn how to follow through and do what's right in our families.

And in chapter 10, we'll learn how to build a dependable friendship with our spouse that can last a lifetime.

Together, we can raise happier kids by staying more happily married. Let's get to it!

# Part 3

# THE SOLUTION:
# TO RAISE HAPPY KIDS,
# PUT YOUR MARRIAGE FIRST

# Chapter Six

# The Grass Is Not Greener: You've Already Chosen Your Ideal Mate

After they'd been married a few months, Ron and Jennifer started to become aware of a few personality traits they'd never noticed before in each other.

Ron had always admired Jennifer's strength and independence. She was already a high-level executive at a well-known company, and it seemed like she was on the fast-track to career success. But Ron had never noticed how uptight Jennifer could be. She obsessed about details that didn't bother Ron before they moved in together. She worked long hours, and when she did come home, she seemed so wound-up that it was hard to get her to relax. Ron wondered if he'd made a mistake. Sure, it was nice to have a successful wife, but did it mean he'd spend the rest of his life with an uptight woman who could never kick back and actually *enjoy* life? Perhaps in the long run it was more important to choose somebody fun-loving than successful. . . .

Jennifer had always admired Ron's charisma. He had a dynamic, take-charge personality, and he really lit up a room. But Jennifer had never noticed how critical and judgmental Ron could be about just the little everyday things of life. It seemed he was always taking issue with the way she drove or the way she handled herself at parties when they went out. Jennifer wondered if she'd made a mistake. Ron's charisma was wearing thin on her, given all the little barbs and criticisms she now had to endure. She wished she had chosen a kinder, gentler man instead of the life of the party. How could she handle the next forty or fifty years with Ron?

Have you ever secretly wondered whether you married the wrong person? This chapter will put your mind at peace. We will address Myth #3, mentioned in the introduction: "If we feel unfulfilled in our marriage, it's because we married the wrong person." Here are the five key points we'll cover:

1. Sexual "chemistry" is Mother Nature's way of scoping out your perfect mate.

2. We feel chemistry for a mate with the same level of anxiety we have.

3. As cave men, our survival depended on finding a mate with the same level of anxiety.

4. Mother Nature's chemistry doesn't lie: you may think, "I'm laid back and my spouse is uptight," but you're not more mature than your mate, so accept him and commit to creating a good marriage.

5. Even if your "next" spouse could miraculously turn out to be Prince Charming, we drag our anxious baggage into all relationships.

These points are crucial because many spouses today secretly wonder if they're unfulfilled because they married the wrong person. We harbor a secret illusion that we may be superior to our spouses, and the "grass would be greener" with a new partner. This nagging, secret doubt erodes our commitment to our marriages, so this chapter will help us let go of that illusion and recommit to our marriages.

It's actually great news that we're no better than our spouses, because it simplifies our lives. Any sense of superiority is a delusion that causes tremendous unhappiness in a marriage. Our goal is no longer to find a better offer and upgrade. Instead, we can finally take our eyes off the exit door and focus our attention on improving our existing marriages.

In this chapter we will come to understand how Mother Nature already chose the perfect spouse for us. When we feel chemistry for someone, that's a sign we've found a compatible mate, both in terms of personality traits and the degree of emotional baggage they carry.[1] Chemistry doesn't lie, no matter how much we wish to convince ourselves we got a raw deal.

Sure, we all know people who say their second marriage is better, but in the great majority of cases, it's not because they chose wrong the first time. In this chapter we'll learn how chemistry brought them together, but their baggage drove them apart.

If their second marriage is happier, it may be because their level of commitment to making it work is higher. If our first marriage doesn't work out, it's easy to assume we chose the wrong mate and to blame our ex-spouse. But if our second marriage doesn't work out, we are forced to take a profound, painful look at ourselves. That's why psychiatrists note that people in their second marriage tend to be far more determined to make that marriage work. For those whose second marriage is better than their first, perhaps they are desperate to avoid a second heartache, so their determination is a primary factor in their success the second time around.[2]

Of course, there are also those rare few who stopped blaming their ex and learned from the painful mistakes of their first marriage, so they became attractive to a more mature spouse the second time around.

For the rest of us, the facts speak for themselves. We may believe we'd choose better next time, but, as we have seen, the divorce rate for second marriages is 60 percent, and for third marriages it's 73 percent. If we married a new partner tomorrow, we'd still carry all our personal baggage into that relationship too, whether we're aware of it or not.[3] So let's learn to accept the marriage we're in by learning how Mother Nature's chemistry got us here in the first place.

## Chemistry: A Primal Instinct between Mates

Many of us like to believe our choice of mate was a thoughtful, rational selection process. But was it, really? Sure, part of the attraction process is conscious: shared interests, similar socio-economic backgrounds, and so on. But then why, for example, do good girls tend to fall for bad boys?

Many of us wish to believe that we are somehow above animals and able to make our choices based on reason, and yet modern neuroscience confirms that the brains of all mammals, ourselves included, evolved from the same stock. Humans are better at controlling and suppressing our emotions, but beneath that thin veneer of civility, we have the same intense, primal emotions that drive much more of our behavior than we realize — including chemistry.[4]

History is rife with stories of sober, responsible young men and women who ignored the advice of their relatives and chose a mate who left their family aghast. The drive to reproduce is primal, but we don't realize that our choice of mates is also primal. That explains why our romantic choices are so often irrational.[5] Chemistry originates in the most ancient parts of our brain, which we share with other mammals. So regardless of what good advice the rational part of our brains may be giving us, when it comes to romantic impulses, our primal instincts still run the show.[6]

We know chemistry when we feel it. It's a very pleasant feeling of being "in synch" with a potential mate. Attunement, as I discussed in chapter 2, is another form of chemistry. In fact, the feeling of chemistry might be similar to the attunement we felt with our first love, our primary caregiver.[7] But what causes our brains to feel chemistry for a particular person?[8]

As two potential mates size each other up instinctively in a few seconds, there's one particular trait in their chemistry that they're not even aware of. People feel chemistry for a potential mate with the same level of anxiety.

Here's a couple of simple proofs:

Picture the "Mr. or Miss Perfect" that you fantasize about. If I waved a magic wand and *poof!* they appeared before your eyes right now . . . would they be attracted to you? My guess is that most of us dream of partners who would never settle for us, even if we did meet them at the Royal Ball, like Cinderella. I guess that seems like bad news for your fantasy life, but it's great news for your marriage and your family, because you can stop eyeing the nearest "Exit" door.

Here's another proof: Back when you were single, did you ever date someone who you intuitively felt was out of your league? When it comes to selecting a potential mate, our intuition is a powerful force, and a mate's level of anxiety may be a bigger factor in chemistry than we realize.

## Similar Levels of Anxiety

Whereas today we may be completely unaware that we choose a spouse with matching anxiety levels, for our ancestors it was a matter of life and death.

As we explored in chapter 5, anxiety is more than a nervous feeling. It is a natural survival instinct within us. Mother Nature gave us the anxiety we needed to protect our families in an era when the stakes were high, and we faced brutal threats on a daily basis.[9] When we left our jungle home and began to adapt to living in open grasslands, we were extremely vulnerable as a species. No longer could we climb a tree for protection, so we needed razor-sharp instincts to help us escape becoming another animal's breakfast. Pack-hunting hyenas, all kinds of big cats, and other animals kept us constantly on our toes.[10]

So our "guardian instinct" of anxiety was nature's brilliant evolutionary solution to survival, because it enabled us to scan the environment for predators or enemies, always trying to anticipate potential threats before they happened.

Today, humans are no longer prey, but our anxiety still acts as if we were. Our level of inner anxiety determines how we react to other people: whether we attack, counterattack, or avoid them.

Since our anxiety has a big influence over how we behave, Mother Nature made sure we instinctively selected a mate who had a similar perception of the imminence of threat.[11] A pair-bond is more durable if it combines like-minded people who react in similar ways to a threat. For example, if one partner is jumpy and quick to overreact to every noise in the bushes, while his or her mate remains relaxed until the last possible moment, those two would be less compatible. As we'll discuss below, choosing a spouse with matching anxiety levels used to be essential in order for us to survive and protect our families.

Back when the stakes were high, Mother Nature provided us the necessary radar equipment in our minds to be able to scope out the right mate. It is the human ability to understand the thoughts, emotions, and intentions of others — to "read" a fellow being, as it were. Our cave man ancestors needed to read others well in order to appraise potential mates and choose the right one for them. Their ability to read others well was an essential survival trait, and this is what gave birth to what we call chemistry.[12]

So where do we get this ability to read others? As we discussed in chapter 2, it begins with our ability to read and relate to our first love, our mothers. Our attunement to our mothers sets the blueprint for our attunement with our future lovers. But how does our brain search out which partners we can feel the deep attunement of chemistry with?

## Our Startle Reflex

The link between attunement and feeling chemistry is empathy. Today, we think of empathy as a warm, fuzzy emotion, like compassion. But the roots of empathy actually go back to anxiety.

Empathy evolved as a fundamental survival instinct. In our cave man days, empathy didn't start out as concern for another's welfare; it began as *distress caused by another's distress*. Primitive empathy allowed us to feel what our neighbor was feeling, so if our neighbor felt threatened by danger, we could also be on alert. Empathy is what made anxiety so contagious, because it helped communicate danger throughout the whole herd *fast*.

In chapter 5, we discussed how mirror neurons made anxiety highly contagious, because a startled reaction was quickly mirrored by all the animals in the herd, setting off a stampede to escape. Even today, that "mirrored distress" response can spread anxiety from person to person like wildfire, because when someone next to us is feeling anxiety, it tends to evoke anxiety in us too.[13]

Mother Nature hard-wired us to dislike witnessing the pain of others. For example, young children will get upset and run back to their mothers when they see another child start to cry. It's not so much that they feel sorry for the other child as they feel overwhelmed by the feelings it evokes in their own minds. As primatologist Frans de Waal observes, empathy means that others' emotions tend to arouse similar emotions in us, "from laughing and joy to the well-known phenomenon of a room full of crying toddlers. We know now that emotional contagion resides in parts of the brain so ancient that we share them with animals as diverse as rats, dogs; elephants, and monkeys."[14]

In our cave man days, we felt chemistry and compatibility with someone who reacted to the world (and its threats) with the same level of intensity. It's hard to maintain a relationship if you're constantly on the lookout for attack while your spouse casually lounges in the sun, or vice versa. A couple with similar perceptions of threat would get along more smoothly in procreation and protecting their family. Hence, our ancestors felt chemistry for a partner with the same level of anxiety, because it meant their partner would have a similar threshold for triggering their fight-or-flight response. In moments of danger, there was no time for second-guessing, so it was an evolutionary advantage to have a mate who perceived threats with the same level of intensity.

Today, choosing a potential mate with the same level of anxiety is no longer a matter of life or death. But our brain has yet to receive that memo. Evolution changes things very slowly, and we approach modern relationships with some outdated equipment in our brains. We still feel chemistry for potential mates at roughly our same level of anxiety, according to the research of psychiatrists Murray Bowen and Michael Kerr.[15]

When we're dating, what we call "chemistry" is a feeling of harmony, or being in synch with our partner, and it's probably because our mirror neurons mimic our mates in several unconscious ways: we may share similar attunement patterns from when we were infants with our mothers, so as adults these patterns now mesh nicely. Feeling in-synch may also stem from similar patterns of empathy or "shared distress," and similar patterns of perceiving what is a threat. In short, if we have similar thresholds for triggering our fight-or-flight response, we may feel compatible.

At this point, I can certainly understand if you're surprised to read that our level of anxiety plays a big role in who we feel chemistry for and choose as mates. It's certainly not the image we hold of ourselves when we decide whom to marry. However, there is compelling evidence for the importance of chemistry and anxiety in choosing a mate, based on a recent survey of women around the world.

Women in thirty-seven cultures were asked to rank the qualities they most desired in a husband. Chemistry ranked number one. Above all, these women saw mutual attraction as essential to their marriages.

The next top traits after chemistry were a dependable character, emotional stability, maturity, and reliability.[16] None of the women surveyed said they seek a man with the same level of anxiety.

And yet, consider what the above-mentioned traits have in common: emotional stability and maturity imply an ability to self-regulate, and control one's emotions. A man with high anxiety will be more trigger-happy, overreacting to situations and triggering his fight-or-flight response more often. Such a man may be less stable emotionally, and may act out in immature ways. Furthermore, dependable character and reliability also imply an ability to stay calm and steady in the midst of life's storms, so a less anxious man may be calmer.

One may conclude that in fact a man's level of anxiety is the common denominator in all four of the traits women say they most desire in a husband. When we say we seek a like-minded mate who shares our outlook on life, we may not have realized it until now, but our level of anxiety and what we react to is a big factor in determining our outlook on life. In my assessment, the above survey provides compelling evidence that Murray Bowen and Michael Kerr are right, and we feel chemistry for a mate who matches our level of anxiety.[17]

That doesn't mean that couples handle their anxiety in identical ways. Looks are deceiving, so we can't judge a book (or a couple) by its cover. Remember Sabrina from chapter 1, who projects anxiety onto Ian "because of his cough" while her husband distances? Or Bob and Jackie, who blame each other at the company barbeque in chapter 3. And in this chapter, Jennifer tends to be obsessive while Ron tends to be critical. I believe each person has the same level of anxiety as his or her spouse; they just deal with it in different ways. So opposites may well attract, at least in terms of outward personality traits, but the level of inner anxiety is the same in both spouses.[18]

Mother Nature created chemistry to make sure we chose the right mate, thus increasing the survival and reproduction of humans. But in modern society, under rule of law, humans are no longer prey. Chemistry may no longer be a matter of survival, but it still dictates compatibility. For example, a low-anxiety person is unlikely to be attracted to a high-anxiety person. If Mahatma Gandhi were alive today, he might feel compassion for a guest on *Jerry Springer,* but he'd be unlikely to marry her. High-anxiety people may feel uncomfortable around or intimidated by lower-anxiety folks, who are unlikely to be attracted to anxious people who have more drama in their lives.

## What Brings Us Together
## Also Drives Us Apart

The anxiety factor in chemistry explains why a couple with higher anxiety in their marriage encounters a lot of drama.

In a sense, they are stuck in fight-or-flight mode, and unconsciously seeks someone to fight with (or flee from). People with higher anxiety perceive more threats in their lives more often and tend to act as if they're in life-and-death situations when, objectively speaking, they are not. If both spouses have a high level of anxiety, they will have a greater tendency to attack or avoid each other.

The anxiety factor in chemistry also explains why good girls fall for bad boys. The good girls may seem more mature because they follow the rules, are successful by society's standards, and seek to please others. We often perceive good girls as the victims of the bad boys, who are the "villains." But if these good girls were actually more able to control their anxiety than the bad boys they crave, they would immediately sense the drama ahead and stay away.

However, the good girl can't help herself, no matter how hard her friends and family try to warn her.[19] She seeks the bad boy because she has just as much anxiety, which means she is just as addicted to the drama as he is, and she contributes to the drama just as much as he does, albeit less visibly. If you remember our discussion in chapter 3 about blamers and self-blamers, you'll understand that the stereotypical good girl is a self-blamer. She seeks to please because it's so painful when someone finds fault with her. The stereotypical bad boy is a blamer. His battles with authority or his mistreatment of his wife are examples of how he always manages to find fault with the *other* person — never his own behavior.

Most of our marriages are not that extreme, but we all share the same anxious tendency to blame our spouse or allow our spouse to join us in blaming ourselves — it's just a matter of degree. Thus, even if one spouse appears mature while the other does not, under the surface they both carry the same level of anxiety. Otherwise, they wouldn't have felt chemistry for each other in the first place.

So having the same level of anxiety is a major factor in the chemistry we feel for our mate. But once chemistry has brought us together, that same level of anxiety in both spouses is what can drive us apart. If you remember the "boiling pots" metaphor in chapter 5, when two people with half-full pots marry, suddenly their combined pot is full almost to the brim. This combined anxiety can manifest itself in a marriage as an argumentative fight response, or a distancing flight response. It's up to us to learn how to handle that anxiety as constructively as possible.

## Chemistry Doesn't Lie, So Accept Your Mate

The inevitability of chemistry and our mating instinct may seem like bad news. In fact, it's great news: now you know how Mother Nature guarantees we choose the right mate by the chemistry we feel for him. This chemistry obviously benefits our species, or else we wouldn't have evolved this way. So we fare better when we give up the illusion that the grass is greener and there *must* be a better mate out there waiting for us. This insight can offer you incentive to accept yourself and your spouse as you are.

Mother Nature doesn't lie. You married a spouse who matches your level of anxiety. If you were to remarry, you'd probably find a spouse without the traits you so reacted to in your first marriage, but their underlying level of anxiety would be the same. And you would drag all of your baggage into the next marriage as well. Things might *seem* different, but the basic coping mechanisms of blame, fight, or distancing are always beneath the surface — it's just a matter of which gets more use in your new relationship. So the grass may not turn out any greener on the other side.

It's likely that there are hundreds, perhaps thousands of "soul mates" out there for each of us. To think there's only one person out there for each of us defies reality. Otherwise, why would anyone remarry? We (and our chemistry instincts) simply picked a mate with a similar level of anxiety, who happened along at the right time, and the hormones flooding our brains convinced us that this person was The One.

The surprising truth is that Mother Nature created the "chemistry" of romantic attraction to ensure you married your ideal mate. So finding your perfect partner is really a matter of seeing your current partner in a different light. You'll be amazed at the sense of relief you'll feel when you eliminate your longing for greener grass.

## Playing the Hand We Were Dealt

In life, our family has dealt us the hand we are playing. Some cards are aces, and some are just deuces. The problem is that we sometimes beat ourselves up or blame others if our hand is crummy. In fact, most of your hand was dealt before you were old enough to have any say in the matter. Your family has its habitual ways of acting, reacting, and overreacting, and your family members began to subtly, unconsciously imprint the family's behavior on you from the day you were born.

This raises the question: why would our family "deal crummy cards" to us, and pass on its bad habits for handling life? The answer is that they don't even realize they're doing it, because humans are herd animals, and attunement with our parents and other family members leaves a deep impression on our behavior.

As we discussed in chapter 5 on anxiety, herd animals tend to follow and imitate the behavior of their family and peers. Gazelles teach their young how to escape a predator at all costs, even if it means leaving a sibling to its death. Our chimpanzee cousins teach their young how to bite the testicles off of defeated males during wars over territory. And some humans teach their male offspring "not to take any crap" from anyone else, so they end up escalating an argument when it would have been better to walk away. Other young human females observe their fathers treating their mothers badly. Later, they find themselves strangely attracted to the "bad boy" type of man.

The herd instinct, imprinting, and attunement are powerful forces in humans. We like to kid ourselves that we're completely independent individuals who think for ourselves, but that may be living in denial. Only when we become aware of the anxiety and imprinting that influences our behavior can we begin to change it. You can't change what you can't see.

There are many factors that influence the hand you were dealt in life. You had no control over many of them. It's easy for humans to see how we had no control over our family's race, or what country we were born in. It's harder for us to see how the herd instinct of our families and communities played a huge role in shaping our behavior.

The hand you've been dealt is just as random as five cards coming out of a dealer's deck in Vegas. The behaviors and habits you use in life were hard-wired into you by your family of origin. We can debate whether it was genetics or nurture that shaped your personality, but that doesn't change the cards you're holding in your hand now.

Likewise, your parents didn't mean to pass down their nasty temper or their anxious fretting habits to you. Those were just the cards dealt to them by their previous generation, and they were playing the hand they were dealt. That's why your parents are not to blame. They were just doing the best they could. And you can criticize or be bitter about how they messed you up, but that's just armchair quarterbacking.

You didn't deal yourself your hand, your family did. As Dr. Murray Bowen used to say, "You've inherited a lifetime of suffering. Go out and do the best you can with it." He didn't mean that we inherit our family's baggage genetically. It's not genetic; it's more about nurture than nature. He meant that growing up in the environment of our family leaves a tremendous imprint on us, and that's the "hand we're dealt" by our families.

This insight can miraculously shift your perception of yourself. Before, you may have thought you were the problem — perhaps feeling ashamed of your character defects. Now you can see the problem originates in your family, and you're just playing the (rather difficult) hand you were dealt.

Relief! Shame and guilt washed away! You're not a bad person because you have this or that character defect. You may be stuck with this hand, and you may have wanted a different hand, but we don't pick our families. So it's not about the quality of your hand. Some people were dealt better hands than us, but many people were dealt worse hands. What matters is how well we play our hand.

So no one is to blame, and there's tremendous freedom in that. But instead of blaming or seeing ourselves as victims, we can choose to take responsibility for playing our hands the best we can. And there's tremendous power in that.

Ask any poker player, and she can tell you how players with weak hands can often win the whole pot. Likewise, players often throw in their hands when it actually would have been a winner.

Much of human behavior has already been "hard-wired" by the time we reach adulthood. But even a slight change in your tendency to overreact will dramatically alter the course of your life. To return to my favorite metaphor, think of your life's path like a ship's voyage across stormy waters: if we change course by only one degree, over time the ship ends up in calmer seas. Likewise, if we shift our brain's reaction patterns by just 1 percent, over time it changes our entire life's course. We can end up in much calmer, "warmer waters" than originally charted.

There's tremendous simplicity to be gained when you stop splitting your focus between your current spouse and the one you wish you had. When you can simply focus on the spouse in front of you and realize he's the one, and you're not missing anything, then you can commit to your marriage on a level you may have never experienced before. You remember the old saying, "I'll believe it when I see it"? In marriage, you'll see it when you believe it. When you commit to your relationship and remove all the exits, you'll be amazed at what you can build with all of your energy focused in one direction.

Many couples I talk to recognize that their marriage is slowly going bad, but they don't know how to change it. What can couples do to turn things around? The answer is to learn how anxiety controls so much of our behavior. The only reason your partner isn't already perfect may be more about your own perceptions rather than his or her actual flaws. Once you learn how to control and reduce your anxiety, you will increasingly accept what used to bug you about your partner (and about yourself). In order to rise above the ugly behaviors of our instincts, we humans have to train ourselves to recognize when we attack or avoid our parents, spouses, and children. Instead of becoming experts on how our spouse criticizes or avoids us, we need to become experts about ourselves and our own habits, behaviors, and reactions. That's what we'll focus on in the next chapter.

## Chapter Seven

# Take a Crash Course
# on Your Family's History
# So You Don't Repeat It

Alan and his mother haven't gotten along well for years, and there's a lot of bad blood between them. They both have excellent justifications for why the breach is the other person's fault; both have plenty of blame to place.

In their conversations, one of them is constantly attacking, counterattacking, or justifying his or her behavior. They are blind to this pattern, because their fight-or-flight instinct has taken over.

Alan is so reactive around his mother that it feels better (and seems prudent) just to avoid her. This is Alan's flight response: he escapes either physically (by not calling) or emotionally (by not discussing any personal or sensitive topics when they talk).

Does this sound like anyone you know?

As we learned in chapter 3, the reasons Alan or his mother might give for their conflict only mask the underlying anxiety that locks them into what I call the Blame Game. The real reason the two of them don't get along is that when Alan and his mom are together, they are hypervigilant, each with their fingers on the trigger of fight-or-flight mode. They both have high anxiety to begin with, and on top of that, they've got *history,* which predisposes them to overreact to each other. Alan's mother doesn't *cause* his anxiety; it's already within him. This chapter is about learning how to recognize when you're stuck in the Blame Game.

But Alan is trying to break free of his fight-or-flight instinct. He notices one day, as he and his wife, Debbie, are on their way to meet his mother, that Debbie seems to be doing a lot of annoying things and making mistakes. He thinks his criticism of Debbie is justified, but in fact, he's acting out of the anxiety that's building within him as he anticipates being in the same room with his mom. This anxiety has heightened his irritability, so little things Debbie does seem like a big deal to him. Debbie's behavior, in fact, hasn't changed.

Now here's Alan's first big step of progress: he catches himself snapping at Debbie, and realizes, "Hey — I'm focusing a lot on Debbie's behavior. Whenever I'm finding fault with others and getting upset, that's usually a red flag that I'm anxious about something. I wonder what that could be...."

Alan's noticing of his criticism is a giant step forward for his relationships, with both his wife and his mom. He is beginning to notice how his family history is affecting his marriage, and this is a first and major step toward changing his negative behavior.

In this chapter, we "go on safari" to observe the herd that is our family of origin. Going on safari allows you to take a crash course in your family dynamics, which empowers you to learn from your family's mistakes and do things differently in your own life. Specifically, we'll look at your family's anxiety and imprinting (as discussed in chapter 5).

We're going to explore stories of people who reaped some very practical benefits from going on safari. Here are three of those benefits:

1. You can better accept your loved ones: When you criticize others, it's a red flag that you're anxious about something and your own irritability is boiling over onto others. The best place to work on reducing your anxiety is in your relationships with your parents and siblings.

2. You can improve your behavior: The way you act in your family of origin is the way you act in all your relationships. If you research your family's imprinting process, you'll learn where some of your flaws came from and how to improve them.

3. You can improve your marriage and parenting: If you learn how to manage the anxiety in your relationship with your parents, it will have a ripple effect through your other relationships.

Going on safari is crucial because as you reduce your anxiety, you reduce the drama with your loved ones. This has a ripple effect of making all your relationships less anxious, with less blaming and distancing.

Here's how going on safari in your family is different from anything you've done before: The goal here is a new kind of self-awareness and simplicity. Society has taught us that self-awareness involves "becoming aware of your feelings." I say it doesn't matter if you can distinguish ten different shades of anger, or if you can tell "apprehension" from "fear." Our feelings are like the weather: difficult to predict and constantly changing. Instead, let's look at what lies at the root of our anger and fear. The common denominator is anxiety.

As we will see in this chapter, if you learn to notice your anxiety, you can reduce your feelings of anger and fear, since it is anxiety that triggers fight or flight. The best training ground for noticing your anxiety is your parents and siblings. It was through your attunement with them, and their imprinting on you as a child, that you acquired your level of anxiety in the first place. So the more you study your relationships with them, the more you learn about your relationships with everyone else in your life.

What does it mean to go on safari in your family? Think of Jane Goodall and her amazing studies of chimpanzees in Africa. Her patient observation of those chimp families yielded fascinating insights into one of our closest cousins. Going on safari means becoming Jane Goodall (a detached, objective observer of primates) and getting to know your family history. You're looking for patterns of behavior that indicate pockets of high anxiety — what pushes the buttons of your relatives. But most important of all, you are observing your interactions with them. Specifically, you are noticing when your anxiety spikes in an interaction with a family member.

The self-awareness I'm talking about doesn't mean noticing your anxiety as you meditate alone in a room. It means noticing your anxiety as you interact with your family members *in real time*. You can develop the ability to observe what's going on in your head even as you speak to them, and even as you listen to their response.

In other words, you are learning to notice the rise and fall of anxiety within your mind as you interact with family members. This practice yields several benefits, which we will explore in turn.

## Benefit #1: Accepting Your Loved Ones

Our example of Alan and Debbie from earlier in this chapter illustrates this benefit beautifully. Alan thought Debbie was making a lot of mistakes, which justified his feeling irritable and critical of her. But Alan was learning to notice his anxiety in himself, and he remembered that criticism is often an indicator of underlying anxiety. When he started scanning his brain for anxiety, he realized that his upcoming visit with his mother had probably spiked his anxiety and rendered him irritable.

Do you see what a breakthrough that is? In this situation, most people would blame their spouse for their bad mood. Instead, Alan realized the real cause of his bad mood was anxiety stemming from his relationship with his mom. This realization reduced the drama with his wife and helped him to better prepare for his visit with his mother. Awareness of our anxiety is incredibly empowering.

At first, it will be easier to notice your heightened anxiety/ irritability in the hours leading up to a stressful meeting with a family member. The act of just noticing your anxiety will lower it, and you'll be able to approach your meeting more thoughtfully and resourcefully. Or you may begin to notice how anxious and reactive you are *after* you've left a stressful meeting, in which case you'll be able to recover your inner peace more quickly. That way, you won't spray your anxious reactivity on others by fuming for hours or snapping at your loved ones.

Here's what we're really doing here: by noticing your anxiety, you are changing some of your brain's "hard wiring," the neuronal pathways of your habitual reaction patterns. By using the thinking part of your brain to observe your anxiety more often, you divert more signals away from the instinctive, reptile part of your brain. What used to be a well-worn path from your irritable anxiety to your fight instinct can become a less traveled road.

As you begin to notice your anxiety before or after a stressful interaction, let's say you've "reduced traffic" on this path of conflict by 1 percent. With practice, you can even notice your anxiety during a stressful conversation, which will help you respond thoughtfully perhaps 5 percent more of the time. We can't change most of our family's imprinting, and 5 percent may not sound like much, but imagine how different your life trajectory will be if you overreact to situations 5 percent less: over time, that's a lot more peace of mind.

If you can begin to realize that criticizing your spouse may not be about his or her faults, but actually about your own heightened irritability, you'll get a foot in the door, too. Your automatic fight-or-flight instincts will no longer run the show in your relationships.

For example, in the past you may have thought, "My spouse is making mistakes, and that is the cause of my criticism and irritability toward her." You used to be absolutely sure that your spouse's actions were to blame for your criticism, and you were so certain of this that you never even dreamed of questioning yourself. But with the new perspective, you may think, "Gee, I notice how many times I've snapped at my spouse. I wonder what's at the bottom of my irritability."

That shadow of a doubt, that sliver of uncertainty, is fantastic because it derails the autopilot of your instinctive reactions. The fight-or-flight response never wonders: it simply reacts in a split second. But if you're wondering, it means you're thinking. If you're thinking, it means you're not governed by your instincts alone. And the more you're thinking, the more willful control you have over your behavior. You may even apologize to your spouse by acknowledging your crabbiness and speculating on its probable cause.

Thinking trumps the fight-or-flight response in your brain.

This is your ticket out of the misery of the Blame Game, because it's a change from your amygdala's anxiety-driven reaction to a thoughtful response from your prefrontal cortex, which is the logical, reasonable part of the brain unique to humans. If you are able to observe your mind for even a few seconds as you're on your way to visit your mother (for example), you've made the first step in changing the way you interact with her. When you actually arrive and begin to interact with a parent, you may fall into the same old pattern of fight or flight. But that split second of self-observation before you arrived is the key to change.

Even if you don't think of your current relationship with your primary caregiver as sour, it's a great place to start practicing self-observation. After all, she was your first relationship, your first attunement, and your first source of anxious memories stored in your amygdala.

During the next several visits with your parent, over the next several months, try to increase the number of seconds you spend in self-observation mode. The more you can observe yourself, even in those clutch moments of tension, the more you can control your fight-or-flight response. That means you may find the right thing to say at the right time, because you may be thinking more calmly.

At first you may only be able to observe or notice your anxiety about seeing your mother while you're physically on the way there. When you're actually present with her, your instinctive emotions may run too high for you to be able to observe yourself. If you make a conscious effort, however, you may be able to observe what you're feeling after you've come home from your visit. At this point you can thoughtfully review in your own mind the interactions you had with your mom and pick out places where you "fell off the horse," so you can do better next time.

To sum up Benefit #1: if you notice your anxious reactions to a parent, you can begin to "spray" less anxiety onto your other loved ones, since they may not be the *actual* cause of your anxiety.

One note of caution: this is about working on yourself within your family, not working on changing your family. There is no advantage in telling your family what you're up to, and if you *do* tell them, it will change the dynamic of your interactions with your family. Therefore, I recommend focusing on yourself and not explaining your self-awareness to members of your family of origin.

## Benefit #2: Improving Your Personality

Here's an example of a man who studied his family of origin to reduce his fight-or-flight response with his wife:

Alex had a strange argument with his wife, Isabelle. Their discussion of finances had escalated in tone and intensity until they were just short of yelling. Then Alex began to speak in a slow, quiet voice, such that Isabelle could barely hear what he was saying. The tension went out of the room, and Alex says that suddenly they were able to think clearly instead of just reacting to each other.

Alex's action was remarkable. Somehow he was able to adopt a quiet, gentle voice, even as he was boiling over inside. His quiet words stopped the escalation and prevented both spouses from stubbornly digging in their heels. But in the heat of the moment, how was he possibly able to do that?

One day Alex told me very candidly that he was often surprised at the difficulty he has in getting along with people. He saw himself as being very reasonable and logical with others, and defending himself only when things went bad. He said he could sense that people felt very resistant toward him. He remarked on the contrast between how smoothly people received his wife and how they would ignore or resist even his most reasonable assertions, no matter how diplomatically he spoke. It was as if his wife was the angel to be received, and he was the demon to be resisted. Alex wondered why.

Together, Alex and I examined his family of origin. I asked him to pick out the relatives he disliked, and identify which trait of theirs irritated him the most. He described one brother who always spoke as if what he said was the irrefutable truth, and if someone disagreed, it was implied they must be blind or stupid. Alex said he clearly sensed his brother spoke that way because he was insecure. He believed that if his brother were truly that sure of himself, then he wouldn't feel compelled to communicate in such a high-handed way. He described his brother's manner as "both tense and *intense.*"

Once he had articulated his sibling's tendency for the first time, he began to notice that this was a trait throughout his entire family, including siblings, parents, and grandparents — it was simply a matter of degree. The siblings who irritated him the most merely had the highest degree of "tense and intense"-ness when they spoke. It wasn't just their words or even just their tone of voice: there was a "vibe" — a kind of palpable intensity in Alex's family members when they related to others.

The French have a wonderful saying, "On prête souvent ses défauts aux autres" (literally, "We often lend our faults to others"). What it means is that we can spot our own faults much more easily in others than in ourselves. What irritates us most about others is often a fault we actually possess in our *own* character. Remember the imprinting we discussed in chapter 5? When Alex spotted a negative trait in some of his siblings, he knew that his family's imprinting meant that he might possess that trait as well. (I'm not saying we have all the negative traits of our siblings, but it's a great place to start looking for insight into oneself.) Once Alex saw that a "tense and intense" trait runs in his family, it wasn't hard for him to realize why he had trouble getting along with others.

You see, that kind of intensity ups the ante in a conversation, and if people feel uncomfortable or threatened in any situation, they're much more likely to dig in their heels and escalate with conflict. Any kind of tension that triggers the human fight-or-flight response is going to make a conversation much more touchy and volatile. Sometimes it's fun to be around intense people, but more often we feel uncomfortable, even if we can't put our finger on why. It's not about the words they choose. Tone of voice is a factor, but the vibe people put off as they communicate is what we "hear" the loudest, even if we can't articulate our impressions very well.

It was fascinating to watch Alex's manner change after he came to that realization. During the first half of our conversation, he was his usual tense, intense self. In the second half, he took on a gentle, agreeable demeanor, and he wasn't faking it. He could truly see how he had been shooting himself in the foot by approaching others in a tense and intense way. He described how his chest seemed to "unclench" as tension drained away. In tense moments, have you ever caught yourself clenching your jaw or tightening your stomach? It was as if Alex noticed for the first time in thirty-some years that both his speech and manner had been clenching, and tight. He said, "I'm sad that it took me thirty-seven years to notice my tense-and-intense manner of relating to others. But I'm *really* glad it didn't take me forty-seven!"

Haven't we all had those "Aha!" moments of maturity, when we see a blind spot in our character for the first time and grow up a little, right on the spot? Alex still has that tendency to be tense and intense, and probably will for life. But now that he's observed that tendency in himself, he has brought a piece of his behavior from automatic knee-jerk into his conscious awareness instead. Notice that Alex wasn't trying to control or change his loved ones. The more control Alex has over his behavior, the more mature and at peace he is as he navigates the shoals of life and relationships. This gives him better results than beating his head against the wall, trying to change others.

We can take back some control of our emotions with the power of self-observation and family observation. We don't have to be dependent on the people around us for how we feel on a given day. We can control more of our fate, and create more of the life we're living — rather than being tossed about on the stormy seas of other people's behavior.

## Let's Go on Safari!

Want to pass on less baggage to your kids? Want to be less overreactive? Put on your Jane Goodall hat, and let's go on safari to your family of origin. Observe a strange herd of humans in their natural habitat, the household. Who are the "alpha" males and females? Who are the outcasts? Where is the tension, competition, or struggle for hierarchy?

Ever since our cave man days, the family we're born into has largely determined how much trigger-anxiety we're hard-wired with. That's why some of us are calm, while others are touchy. Of course, not everyone is affected equally, and some siblings will soak up more of the anxiety than others. But we can all reduce our anxiety by becoming aware of the behavior patterns and roles we play within our family herd, and replacing our knee-jerk reactions with a thoughtful response. If our anxiety level is lowered, then we won't have such an itchy trigger finger on our fight-or-flight response. Thus, we can go through our day more calmly, and can think our way more clearly out of a problem. The more we can control our fight-or-flight response, the less unnecessary drama we have in our lives.

Awareness is the answer. We need to become aware of the imprinting by which a family passes its baggage on from generation to generation before we can change it. We need to observe patterns of behavior in our family that can tip us off to the presence of anxiety.

A key to getting more control over our fight-or-flight response is to begin to see the "Big Picture" of the family we came from. Most of us see only a tiny piece of that picture. Most of us know our parents, siblings, and maybe our grandparents and a few aunts, uncles, and cousins. When we know only about a half-dozen or so members of our family, it's hard to see any patterns. You'd be amazed at the patterns that emerge when you chart your family in one diagram listing each member's job, how many kids they have, and any social or health problems they have.

The more information we can chart about our grandparents (and great-grandparents), the easier it will be to see where our family's negative imprinting and anxious triggerfinger came from. These negative patterns are "red flags" that indicate the anxiety that underlies them.

It's difficult, but the best way to improve your marriage is to work on your knee-jerk reactions with your family of origin. In essence, you're retrenching the neuronal pathways that were carved into your brain as a child by your family's imprinting process. You get a chance to fix the cause of your life's drama, rather than just flailing at the symptoms. The clearer you can get on what your imprinting is and how you ended up with the role you tend to play in your family, the better.

The role you play in your family also tends to be the role you play in life. For example, are you a peacemaker, a rescuer, a black sheep, or do you play some other role in your family of origin? If certain aspects of that role aren't serving you well in life, you can't just wake up one morning and be different. One approach is to go back to your family of origin and change your role as you interact with other family members while they're playing their roles too. As you get clearer on your role in your family and their behavior patterns, you will be able to control your anxiety better in response to family situations.

When you can control your anxiety better, you can change your role in the family for the better, and you'll have the courage to withstand the pressure that family members put on you to change back to the old, familiar way. If you maintain your new, positive role under pressure, you will temper the steel of a stronger, braver character that determines your own direction in life, rather than being blown around by the winds of others. We will discuss this in detail in chapter 9, as it impacts your parenting. You will learn the powerful combination of being calm but firm, clear but flexible, and sure of yourself but able to listen to others.

In summary, here's a strategy for "going on safari" in our families, in order to make progress in reducing our anxiety:

1. Notice a pattern that causes you suffering in life.

2. Research that pattern in your family of origin.

3. Get clear on how the role you play in your family of origin also may be your role in life in general.

4. Become aware of that pattern in yourself as you interact with your family, and work to change it there. The result will be that the pattern will change in all other areas of your life as well.

## Benefit #3: Improving Your Marriage by Working with Your Parents

Here's why any change you make in interacting with your family of origin reaps tremendous benefits:

It's difficult, but if you can break out of your usual pattern of behavior in your family of origin, it affects how you react in all relationships, whether friend or family. In other words, changing one knee-jerk reaction in your family has a ripple effect that cascades through all your relationships. That's why the best way to improve your marriage and how you relate to your children is to work on your knee-jerk reactions with your family of origin.

Think of your interactions with your mother as a kind of dance step that never changes. For example, she plays the martyr, you placate her but feel angry inside, she senses your anger and reacts, you overreact to her reaction, and things escalate. Perhaps you've danced this dance over and over together for years, but it's so ingrained and unconscious that it seems inescapable.

But you *can* learn to notice the dance and stop dancing. Here's how a man named Scott observed a pattern in his family and changed his knee-jerk response into a thoughtful one.

Scott's mother is a seventy-one-year-old widow living in a small cottage in Maine. So when Scott's family visits with his wife and three children, they're usually feeling cramped after a few days, and want to go up to his sister's large house right on Maine's coast.

Scott's mom enjoys herself when she visits her daughter's house, but unfortunately she also has a habitual behavior where she plays the martyr. For example, she often focuses on how she feels rejected that Scott and his family don't stay with her all the time. Rather than saying, "Yes, I'll ride up with you this afternoon," she'll say, in a tone of self-pity, "You guys go ahead and have fun. I'll come up in a few days." That few days will stretch into several days, and then she'll insist on taking the public bus on a four-hour route even though Scott or his sister volunteers to drive the hour to pick her up.

"I don't want to put anyone out," she says.

Scott used to feel both furious and guilty when his mom played the martyr. Then he developed a new way to handle it. He started to plan for the next interaction with his mom. He knew it was coming. Any family gathering usually had one martyrdom incident, which tied him and his siblings in knots for at least an afternoon.

For the next few martyrdom incidents he observed, however, Scott didn't do anything but notice the spike in his own anxiety at his mom's behavior. Scott went quickly to reactivity mode, and it was all he could do not to react. Think of this as him "studying," familiarizing himself with the subject at hand. Scott observed that he habitually had this spike of reactivity within him. He felt flashes of rage and guilt, and then he had an overwhelming urge to explain why his mother was wrong to behave the way she did.

So Scott studied and observed for a while. To use a baseball metaphor, let's say he was watching the tapes of how his opponent plays, and observing her "from the dugout." Now it was time to step up to the batter's box. He was going to swing at a few pitches, and probably strike out. So he made a few attempts to lighten his mood. Instead of giving in to anger and guilt, he made a few awkward jokes.

"Actually, Mom, maybe you should just walk up to Sis's house — the bus is a waste of money!" Or perhaps, "Okay Mom, I promise we won't have any fun until you arrive." Those didn't go over too well with Mom, but he was still jubilant because it was like a base hit: he was starting to pry himself free of the old, automatic response where he would feel angry and guilty, explain to his mom how her behavior was wrong, and upset them both.

Can you see how Scott first observed himself a little better, then controlled himself a little better? This gave him a tiny sliver of confidence that perhaps he could respond differently to this tango that his mom and he had been dancing for years. And once Scott had that sliver of confidence and hope, it made it easier to observe himself more clearly the next time he was in his mom's presence. This in turn made it easier to get unstuck from the anger and guilt reactivity and lighten up the heaviness with some humor that was less of a counterattack on his mom's behavior. Progress!

Fast-forward to Thanksgiving a few years later. The anxiety level of many families rises as they anticipate being together in one room for this annual tradition. Scott's mother felt her share of anxiety, which primed her to overreact to any perceived insult, thus triggering a martyrdom incident and Scott's usual, unconscious dance with his mother.

Scott didn't even realize he had insulted his mother until after she had already begun their traditional dance. Scott's family was staying in their own hotel room, and his wife, Barbara, and he had taken the kids iceskating that morning instead of stopping over at his mom's house. His mom probably expected them, and was surprised they didn't show. His sister was hosting Thanksgiving dinner for their family, and called to ask him to pick up their mom. So Scott called Mom at 2:00 p.m. and told her they'd stop by at 4:30. She said she couldn't be ready by then, because he hadn't given her enough warning.

In his head, Scott was thinking, Huh? She knew they had plans for dinner at his sister's. Although they hadn't set a pick up time, Mom could safely have assumed it would be between 4:30 and 5:30. What's her story?

Fortunately, he had enough experience from previously "watching tapes" of this pattern, with many strikeouts from practice. So he didn't take the bait. He wasn't sucked into his usual anger and guilt. He stayed outside the emotional smoke screen his mother was (unconsciously) churning out. Thus, he could formulate a better response on the spot.

"Okay Mom. Well, I'll pop by around 4:30 and see if you'd like to join us or not."

Base hit for Scott.

Now, the squeeze play: Scott shows up at 4:30. His mother's alone in the house, dressed to go, and mad as hell. "Why didn't you call me earlier to give me enough time? My hair looks like hell, I didn't have time for a nap, and you always think only of yourself!" Scott started to say something, but she snapped, "Oh, let's just drop it!" She put on her coat and boots, stomped out to his car and sat in silence.

Scott got into the driver's seat and started to say something like, "I only got word at two about picking you up," when she bellowed, "God DAMN it, can't you just DROP it?" His wife and kids sat in stunned silence, but his mother got out of the car, went back into the house, and refused to leave again.

Scott walked back in the house, but (for a change) didn't plead or apologize. She said many things about why she was upset, and he repeated them back to her, to show he was listening carefully. Then when she paused, he quietly said, "I understand what you're saying, Mom, but I don't see it that way."

Stunned silence.

Clearly, Scott had just hit a double, so now he had a man on second and third. But his mom's a seasoned pitcher.

"Go ahead then. I'm not coming."

That was a spitball, but it was predictable. Scott knew she'd find a way to punish him for not dancing their usual emotional dance together. Psychiatrist Murray Bowen refers to this as a "change-back," as in, "I want you to change back NOW!" When you are succeeding at extricating yourself from an emotional pattern that's been a habit for years (like a family tradition), old habits do indeed die hard.

Thanks to all his practice, Scott was now able to recognize that his mom was beginning a martyrdom incident. She felt insulted that she hadn't been given enough advance notice, so she was going to stay home alone, rather than join her own family for Thanksgiving dinner.

For a change, Scott didn't swing at her pitch. Fortunately, he'd observed this pattern so many times that he knew the spitball was coming, so he was observing himself clearly enough that he could manage to prevent a spike in reactivity.

Scott calmly told her to give him a call if she changed her mind, and he'd be happy to come pick her up any time. No edge. No sarcasm. Just calm, clear, and firm. He walked out and drove over to his sister's house.

As you can imagine, his siblings were beside themselves when they heard that their mother would spend Thanksgiving alone. The anguish and the pressure on him to do something was enormous. But Scott stayed as calm as he could, and tried to think clearly what to do. Then he asked himself a question that serves him very well in his close relationships: "What's my role in this conflict?" This question is key, because in any tense situation or conflict, one always has a role. He realized that he could have called his mom to tell her not to expect them that morning.

So he picked up the phone and apologized to her for that. By this point, she had calmed down a lot, and wasn't relishing being alone on Thanksgiving.

"Can I come pick you up, Mom?"

"Okay."

And that was it. Two-run homer.

I want to stress that the process described here isn't about distancing yourself from the craziness of your family. It's about being present and accounted for, right in the *middle* of that craziness, without joining in. This isn't some kind of "my way or the highway!" exercise. It's about observing the anxious overreaction in yourself, and slowly reducing that, so that you can respond differently to the anxiety in others.

If Scott hadn't called Mom to apologize for his role in their conflict, his actions would have had a "screw you!" edge to them. But by owning his part in the conflict, while not reacting in his usual way to his mom's behavior, he was emotionally free of the rage and guilt he used to feel when they danced that dance. It didn't matter anymore if she danced that dance on his head every day going forward. Scott was no longer caught up in it. He no longer blamed Mom for "making" him feel angry and guilty. He simply observed his own internal anxious reactions better, which allowed him to manage them better, which allowed him to stay calm regardless of the behavior directed at him.

*That's* power. That's control.

Trying to change the other person's behavior is a dead end. Trying to change how you feel about it is where you can make the most difference in your life. Scott no longer has to forgive Mom for her behavior. He just accepts that that's what she does, and she has a right to do that. It no longer pushes his buttons as much. This process takes time, and it's usually "three steps forward, two steps back." These days though Scott says he is so confident in dealing with such conflicts that he almost looks forward to them, because it means he gets to practice his "emotional baseball"!

Can you imagine the relief that gives him in life? Can you imagine how much drama that removes from his relationships? The work he did with his mother has a ripple effect throughout his relationships with others.

Of course, when an issue arises, the goal is not just to be calmer with one's family members while remaining silent. The goal is to reduce one's knee-jerk anger or fear. A less reactive response will be more thoughtful and constructive.

Experts agree that the more healthy contact we have with our parents, the healthier our relationships.[1] But that doesn't mean the more contact, the better. We have to distinguish between healthy contact and being married to our parents. If we continue to be married to our parents even as adults, that kind of closeness is not constructive. But if we can relate to our parents as equal, independent adults while remaining close to them, then our families become a valuable resource and a source of joy.

At this point you may be asking, "What does his mother's behavior have to do with Scott's relationship with his wife?" The answer is: everything. Scott was able to manage his anxiety and act differently in the face of anxiety in his family. That is to say, he wasn't trying to change his mother, but trying to change himself. Therefore, he felt reduced feelings of blame, anger, and guilt toward his mother, and there is less "emotional gunk" clogging up his relationship with his family of origin. It's as if he retrenched a neuronal pathway in his brain: he had been programmed since childhood to react to his mom's martyrdom with guilt and angry verbal counterattacks.

Now he had a new neuronal pathway, one that simply "doesn't go there" as often. It's not that Scott feels angry and suppresses it. It's not that he feels angry and then forgives his mom later. He no longer feels angry at all; he feels less caught up in his mother's behavior. This gives him simplicity in his other relationships, and the confidence that he can handle himself better in similar situations.

In short, Scott is a little better weaned from his mother, and a little less involved in the Blame Game. He blames his mother less for what he's feeling and accepts her more. He also blames his wife less. Scott's wife has also begun the same kind of observing and managing herself in her own family of origin. More observing and managing means less reactivity and less blame all around.

Weaning ourselves from our parents is a great gift to give our spouse and kids. The goal is to gently wean ourselves from our parents while staying in meaningful contact with them (as in Scott's example). Progress toward this goal will increase the odds that we can stay happily married to our spouses, with less blaming or distancing. On the other hand, Incomplete Weaning leaves us with more anxiety, which means we are more prone to react anxiously to our spouse — either by fighting or fleeing.

As we discussed in chapter 2 on Incomplete Weaning, most of us fall somewhere on the continuum between emotional independence and total lack of emotional weaning. It's just a matter of degree. But the less we were weaned, the more it affects our lives, even as adults, because it increases our anxiety levels. The goal is to further this weaning process ourselves, while staying in meaningful contact with our parents.

If we can increase our weaning from our parents, even just a little bit, it reduces our anxiety and makes us less trigger-happy in our relationships. The less trigger-happy we are, the less we will be tempted to fight with or flee from our spouses. If we distance less from our spouses, we'll marry our kids less, which in turn allows them to gently wean themselves from us while staying in touch. What a great, lifelong legacy of healthy independence to give our children!

## The Joy of Observing Yourself

One of the greatest gifts of human consciousness is that our self-awareness allows us to observe and reflect on ourselves. Quite simply, if you are observing yourself at any given moment, your thinking mind is controlling the majority of your behavior. If you are using your cortex, the "thinking" part of the brain, to consciously scan your mind as to what you're thinking and feeling in a given moment, the reptile part of your brain is not the exclusive governor of your behavior.

Learning to observe our behavior is a gradual process that starts with getting a toehold in our thinking, logical mind. We first have to understand intellectually that much of our behavior is governed by the instinct of fight or flight. That understanding permits us to start to notice our overreactions. At first, it will only be after we cool down or sleep on it that we can view yesterday's behavior with a little more objectivity. As we get better at observing our own behavior, the lag time between reaction and insight decreases. Initially, we may only see our overreactions days (or months) after the fact. With practice, we can recognize our overreacting, blaming tendencies only hours or minutes after the fact. The goal, of course, is to notice when we start to go there and nip our instinctual, negative reaction in the bud before we act.

As we saw in chapter 5 on anxiety, we have to acknowledge the reptile brain's leadership. Drawing on my earlier metaphor for anxiety, we don't want to just boot out the anxious soldier on guard; we still need him. When the city bus is about to hit you or you wake up and smell smoke in the house, you can't take time to make plans. You want a lightning-fast reaction to get you and your herd to safety. Sometimes anger and fear are pretty good motivators to get things done in life. We still need our reptile brains.

Think of our goal as learning to "observe our anger or fear, as it floats (yes, floats) gently past our mind." It's not about deposing a tyrant, but more like increasing the democratic influence of a trusted ally who has our best interests in mind. We'll still leave the life-and-death situations to our reptile brain, with gratitude for a job well done. But in the rest of life's situations, the thinking mind wants more of a say. Here's how we can increase the influence of our thinking minds over our behavior: Our aim is to slow down our knee-jerk reactions.

Think of our fight-or-flight reaction as that nervous solider on guard duty. Like it or not, evolution has helped animals to survive by making sure that their "soldier" is ready to fire at the slightest perception of threat. Our animal instincts have us hard-wired to react in certain ways to certain situations.

But if we can calm that solider down just a bit, then he'll mobilize the troops less often. And how can we train him to be a little less trigger-happy?

Anxiety is the trigger in our brains. Anxiety is the anticipation of a potential threat. If a cave man sees a rumbling cloud of dust approaching, it's his anxiety that gets him safely into the cave before the elephants stampede over his campfire.

But in modern society we're living a lot longer, thanks to medical breakthroughs and the rule of law. So these days, anxiety often leads to overreactions, rather than the life-saving reactions of the good old days. In other words, if we have too much anxiety in our minds, we produce too much anger or too much fear in proportion to the actual degree of threat. We go into "must survive" mode when in fact we'd be better off in "must speak clearly" mode. This is like an itchy trigger finger, poised to fire off an overreaction.

The more often you can observe yourself as you interact with other key family members (i.e., parents and those who irritate us most), the more often you can think before you act. This allows a thoughtful response to trump a knee-jerk reaction. The more you can control your emotions, the easier it is to observe yourself for longer and longer intervals. As you increase your intervals of observing self, it becomes easier to control your emotions, and so on. It's a circle of progress — *spiraling upward!*

Imagine the peace of mind you could enjoy if you felt less anger and reactivity toward your parents. Sure, if you like, you can still assume they were wrong or mistaken about how they raised you, if that somehow serves you. But what if some of their mistakes and shortcomings were the legacy of your ancestors, passed down to them? I don't want to argue about nature versus nurture, but what if observing your parents' negative behaviors in them and in your other relatives left you feeling less blame, and more acceptance for what your parents did or didn't do? What if you could begin to accept their behavior as just "the hand they were dealt"?

I believe that blame and acceptance are mutually exclusive: the less you blame your parents for how you turned out, the more you accept them as they are. Moreover, the more you accept your parents, the less the behavior pattern they exhibit persists in *your* life. When you accept their behavior, it drains away all the bitterness and reactive drama surrounding those behaviors. Like Jane Goodall, you begin to observe your family's behavior patterns more dispassionately, such that they upset you less, and you're left feeling less resentment and blame toward your parents. Thus, your reaction formation against your parents is lessened, and the "buck stops with you." The family's baggage, which has been unwittingly passed down for generations, now stops with you. You will have given your own child more freedom than they'll ever know.

## I Want Inner Peace Now!

Sometimes you may feel discouraged because you want to have inner peace *now,* and the path I am describing is not quick and easy. This path involves touching the most difficult parts of your relationships that may not even be on your radar because they are so ingrained you don't notice them. But your greatest inspiration should be that now you have a clear path to your goal: if you learn to observe and reduce your reactivity while interacting with your family of origin, this reduced reactivity will have a ripple effect in your interactions with your other relationships. Your work becomes a legacy of calm that you pass onto your kids, who will live a better life for your efforts. This strategy requires slow, hard work, but it's so much better than the alternative: a trial-and-error approach to relationships. In the popular movie *Groundhog Day* with Bill Murray, the way he steps in the same mud puddle every day is like the way we react to our family's drama each time we visit them. Haven't you had enough of stepping into the puddle? Let's escape the Groundhog Day Syndrome!

Humans have been challenged by their relationships for millennia. However, thanks to the unique, thinking part of our brain known as the cortex, we humans aspire to something more. Our cortexes make us aware that there's more to life than indulging our animal instincts. Our cortex permits us to see the big picture, to have a vision and goals, and to fulfill them. One could even argue that the human spiritual journey centers on transcending our animal instincts, to act instead for the greater good of humankind.

However, we will never transcend our anxiety by ignorance, or pretending those instincts don't exist. The logical way to make the most of our existence is to acknowledge what we are, and then improve upon it. Of course each human has individual physical and personality traits, as unique as our fingerprints. But the more we learn about the anxiety that drives us to fit in, and the fight-or-flight instincts that drive us apart, the more we can transcend those animal instincts for our own good.

People spend their whole lives looking for peace and happiness. Learning to override our animal instincts by using our cortex to observe ourselves can bring more inner peace. It's not about attaining perfection; it's about making progress. You may never perfect the process of overriding your fight-or-flight instinct in your lifetime, but to improve even slightly will, I believe, yield more peace and happiness in your relationships than any other approach. That's because you're addressing the cause of human suffering — not just the symptoms. Most of us spend our whole lives just flailing hopelessly at the symptoms.

Your progress in this challenge will take place in baby steps. You won't be hitting any home runs here. You'll be lucky not to strike out a dozen times before you get a base hit. The process is simple, but actually doing it (and not giving up) is very hard indeed. I call it Notice and Control. You have to observe a little more of the anxiety inside you (Notice), and then control a little more of your anxiety inside you (Control).

How do humans learn a new skill? The same way we learn poker, chess, or a new language. We read books about it, then practice what we've learned a bit, then read more books with a heightened knowledge, then practice more effectively and acquire that skill more quickly, and so on. Back and forth between study and practice. Between observation and practice. Between noticing and controlling. With practice, you'll ask the right question in your mind several times during your daily interactions, until it becomes second nature and pops into your head at the moment you need it most.

Only the masters at observing self can feel compassion for a person who is verbally attacking them. That compassion may take over a decade to accomplish. Fortunately, even a millimeter of progress improves all our relationships, so our efforts are never wasted. Nonetheless, I foresee that you may become discouraged at what seems like a snail's pace of progress.

Don't beat yourself up.

For those of us who consider life to be a spiritual journey, that journey usually involves learning to accept ourselves and others as we are. If that's the case, then your efforts observing yourself are a central part of your spiritual journey, so there's nothing more important you could be doing, no matter how long it takes.

Here's a strategy to reduce the drama in your family by charting your family of origin. I've broken it down into five main steps, so hopefully it's easy to understand and implement:

1. Write down three of your character flaws, e.g., you have a short temper, are oversensitive to insults, are too clingy in relationships, and so on.

2. Create a chart of your family tree that goes back three generations.

3. Interview your oldest living relatives and gather some data: Start with the basics, like each relative's birth

date, education, career, marriages, kids, and health or social problems. Then, ask which relatives would they describe as short-tempered? Oversensitive? Get details and examples.

4. As you speak to more relatives, two things may occur: (a) patterns of behavior become clear in your family, and (b) you are deepening your rapport with the relatives you discuss this with.

5. These interviews and the chart give you the Big Picture on your family: the more insight you gain on how your family shaped you, the less guilt and denial you feel about your negative behaviors.

Getting the Big Picture helps you stop blaming your parents — a major dead-end and time-waster. It also introduces a healthy doubt into your former "truth" about how "justified" your blame actually is in your relationships.

When you accept your flaws more, (ironically) it's much easier to change them. The more you accept your flaws, the more you accept them in others. The more you accept yourself and others, the less drama in your family!

Making a family chart may seem complex, but all you're really doing is putting your life in perspective. Most of us feel guilty about our shortcomings, and it seems like we're the only ones in the world who have our problems. But when you discover how you're not responsible for the way you turned out, it's a huge relief. Then you can discover the power of rolling up your sleeves, starting wherever you're at, and taking responsibility for what you do and what you feel.

It's okay if you feel overwhelmed. If you are afraid to begin, let me give you the biggest motivation of all: do it for your kids. They'll have a happier life with fewer problems because you'll pass less of the family baggage on to them.

And that's the subject of our next chapter. We're going to learn how to fix problems in our children by fixing them in ourselves.

# Chapter Eight

# Look for the Problem
# in Yourself First

Geoff was a happy eleven-year-old, playing his heart out on the soccer field. Having scored two goals already, he went in hard and took the ball away from one opponent, but another opponent punched him in the head from behind. Geoff got up and hit him back, but somehow the referee and the coach only saw Geoff's hit.

His coach screamed, "Geoff! Get over here, now!" When Geoff's dad, Larry, called out from the sideline that the other kid had hit Geoff first, the coach yelled back, "We'll take care of it, Dad!" The coach took Geoff over so the other boy could apologize to him, but Geoff refused to shake hands. Geoff was upset not only because he had been hit, but because the coach had yelled at him for it.

The coach told Larry that if Geoff didn't shake hands he couldn't stay in the game. Larry was very upset because he felt like Geoff was being blamed for the other boy's terrible behavior. That same boy went on to trip another player, but when Geoff complained to his coach about it, he said, "Keep your mouth shut and score goals."

Harsh, but that's the hard lesson of sports. The player who controls his temper usually wins. Of course, Geoff was absolutely right that the boy shouldn't have hit him, and the coach shouldn't have yelled at him, but Geoff lost his temper, and it took time for him to settle down. He ended up with only two goals that game, whereas he had scored five in the previous game.

But it didn't end there. In the next game, five days later, both Geoff's coach and his dad, Larry, warned Geoff that he was using his elbows too much when he went in to challenge for the ball. But when the opposing coaches said, "Keep your elbows down, Number 10!" Geoff angrily shouted back that he'd done nothing wrong. Five days ago Geoff had been right, but today Larry saw with his own eyes that his son's elbows were up. Geoff's coach called him over, but Geoff shouted at him too.

Geoff apologized after the game ended, but he still honestly believed that he was a victim of all these mean coaches, who weren't seeing things clearly. Larry dressed Geoff down pretty soundly during the ride home, to try to scare him into never doing that again. He said that the young kids' soccer teams get the young, inexperienced referees who make many bad calls. And even the coaches make mistakes, but the worst thing one could do was to get angry and mouth off to them. That wouldn't change their minds. It would only make them angry at Geoff and draw all the focus to his future play.

But long after Geoff was asleep, Larry was still worried sick about it. He was worried that Geoff actually saw himself as a "poor victim of mean people," even though three coaches and Larry agreed that Geoff was pushing with his elbows. Larry was worried that, despite his incredible talent for sports, Geoff's temper would prevent him from ever succeeding.

Which happens to be Larry's greatest personal fear in his own life — his temper. Was history repeating itself? Could Larry do anything about it? He was overwhelmed with anxiety for Geoff, but how could he stop his own greatest fear about anger from becoming a self-fulfilling prophecy in his son?

As parents, most of us can see problems in our kids that we'd like to fix. We'd like to give our kids the best possible launch into the world, so the more we can repair any problems or bad habits, the better. This chapter offers you a surprising strategy to do just that. We'll cover four main points:

1. Define your kid's problem and search for that same problem within yourself.

2. Trace your kid's problem back to its roots in your family of origin.

3. View your child's problem as a sign of anxiety in you or your marriage.

4. Recognize more of your own drama so that you will be less anxious and thus pass less baggage on to your child.

This information offers you two great benefits. Whereas you may have felt powerless to deal with some of your child's problems in the past, this chapter's strategy will help you take at least *some* control of the situation. Secondly, your kids will benefit because now you will feel less anxiety about their problems, and you'll benefit by being less stressed out: double bonus!

# Step 1:
# Define Your Kid's Problem, and Search for That Same Problem within Yourself

We parents dramatically underestimate just how powerful a role the self-fulfilling prophecy plays in our parenting. This chapter will bring us the awareness we need to reduce that negative influence.

To fix a problem in your child, fix it in yourself first. As Carl Jung said, "If there is anything we wish to change in the child, we should first examine it and see whether it is not something that could better be changed in ourselves."[1] In other words, we need to notice that a portion of our child's problem may actually exist in us; if it didn't, we wouldn't worry so much about it.

You may think you are focusing on your child's problem out of love, but it may in fact be out of your own anxiety. When we are anxious, we tend to become oversensitive and obsessive about small problems in our children. This obsessiveness may lead you to focus on the symptoms of your child's problem, rather than treating the cause of that problem, as we discussed with Projection onto Our Child in chapter 1.

To address your child's problem, you first need to recognize that you're worrying about your kid and then ask, "What's going on in me that could be making *me* anxious?"

Returning to our example above of Geoff on the soccer field, Larry had already noticed that he was worried about Geoff's temper, and Larry was aware of his own temper. In fact, it was *because* of Larry's suffering with his own temper that he was particularly worried about history repeating itself in his son. Larry was oversensitive to the slightest sign of a temper in Geoff, and he overreacted to any anger Geoff showed. Larry further recognized that he was blowing Geoff's anger out of proportion. By creating so much emotional drama around the issue, Larry ended up actually *reinforcing* the behavior that he sought to reduce in his son.

What we resist persists, and this is especially true with parenting. The more we anxiously obsess about or angrily scold a child's behavior problem, the more we create a self-fulfilling prophecy.

There are three main ways that parents deal with a child's behavior problem. The first way is to pour emotion all over the problem by overreacting with anger or anxiety, which creates more amygdala memories of the behavior, deepening the neuronal pathways that created the undesirable behavior in the first place. An animal trainer succeeds by rewarding desirable behavior and acknowledging, but not overreacting to, bad behavior.

Some parents have taken this to an extreme, where they ignore their child's bad behavior. This second way to deal with a child's problem is actually a form of denial. It seems calm on the outside, but the parents' anxiety within is so high that they are denying the problem as a kind of flight response. There are situations where the child must be disciplined and taught the right way to act, and denial is a slippery slope.

The third way of addressing a child's bad behavior is calm, but firm. We don't deny there's a problem, we don't overreact emotionally to the problem, but we acknowledge the problem and define the consequences for it. We'll examine how to do this in chapter 9.

The soccer field incident is just one example of the subtle yet significant ways that Larry and his wife, Tara, are passing on their anger baggage to their kids. They are hypersensitized to any anger Geoff expresses. Geoff's sister can say something rude or throw a tantrum, and Larry and Tara are likely to forget it as soon as it's over. But if Geoff has an angry outburst, his parents jump on it like it's a felony. They respond angrily to Geoff's anger, or they tell him to calm down (does it actually make anyone calmer to hear that?), or they embark on a lecture about how it's important to learn how to control one's emotions, as if they were therapists and Geoff was their twenty-year-old client.

Why can't Larry and Tara just let a kid get angry from time to time, as kids have always done? The answer is that they fear the anger in themselves, so they fear the anger in their kids. But reacting fearfully to anger only makes it worse. By increasing the emotionality around Geoff's alleged anger problem, they actually breathe life into the issue.

This is like the self-fulfilling prophecy I described above and in chapter 1. If parents focus on a child's problem while anxiously wringing their hands, they increase the likelihood the child's shortcoming actually will become a problem. They want what's best for their kids and they have the best of intentions, but they are often blind to the role they play in creating the problems that their children face.

The old saying goes, "When you point the finger at someone else, notice that your other three fingers are pointing back at you." In other words, you think you're objectively perceiving your child's problem. In fact, the problem may lie within you, and you're projecting it onto her without even realizing you're projecting.

## Step 2:
## Trace Your Kid's Problem Back to Its Roots in Your Family of Origin

Once Larry and his wife realized the drama they were heaping on this already difficult problem, it didn't take long to see why they might be sensitized to this issue. They both had their own history of parents with tempers. Here's what Larry and his wife discovered when they went on safari in their families of origin:

Larry's father was a farmer. He used to curse at objects more than at people, but it was still terrifying. Larry can remember the spitting rage in his voice as he screamed at a broken tractor or a stubborn cow, "God, *damn* my soul to hell!" and so on. Little Larry dared not move, while praying quietly, "God, *please* don't send Dad to Hell! He doesn't mean it! Please don't make him burn!" To his credit, Larry's dad never lifted a finger toward his mom or his siblings. But Larry's childhood household lived in fear of his father's outbursts, and his family would do anything to avoid one.

Ever since, when someone tries to dominate Larry with anger, he cowers with fear and wonders what he did wrong.

Larry's wife, Tara, had a mom who used to get so enraged that she would shake her hands in silent fury and stomp away from her family. Tara remembers one family vacation where she and her siblings had been fighting in the back of their minivan. When the van stopped, Tara's mom said she'd had enough and stomped away from the car as if she was leaving for good.

Tara remembers feeling terrified. Rather than talking with his wife or addressing the outbursts constructively, Tara's father reinforced them to the children by telling them they had better behave, or else Mommy would leave them for good. Ever since, Tara has either suppressed her anger and gotten sick, or exploded and stomped off, slamming doors in furious silence.

Larry and Tara didn't want to pass their anger baggage on to Geoff. They wanted him to learn how to handle his anger with moderation: a middle ground between furious outbursts or cowardly suppression. Their research into how their families of origin dealt with anger helped Larry and Tara to understand how their fear of anger was influencing their overreactions to anger in their son. For the first time, they could see how the anxiety and overreaction they attached to Geoff's outbursts actually made them worse. It's a little bit like angrily shouting, "Don't get so angry!" It triggered everyone's reactivity, which drew more attention and emotional intensity to the problem. This emotional intensity is like glue that imprints more negative memories more deeply in Geoff's amygdala, which primes him to overreact even more in the future.

However, tracing your child's problem back to your family of origin can help you begin to notice and reduce the drama you attach to your child's problem. Of course, there's not always a clear link between your child's problem and behaviors in your family of origin. In that case, you can strive simply to reduce the anxiety in your household, which also will reduce your child's problem.

# Step 3:
# View Your Child's Problem
# as a Sign of Anxiety in You or Your Marriage

When your child gets sick or seriously acts out, it's a red flag that something needs attention in your marriage or in your own life. You can learn to view your child as the "identified patient" who bears the symptoms of your own personal problems or marital discord, so then her symptom becomes a wake-up call instead of a nightmare. Perhaps you and your spouse are under pressure, and it's spreading to your kids now. Humans are herd animals, and anxiety is highly contagious — it can easily spread from you to other members of your family via attunement. As we saw in chapter 1, you may be projecting your own problems onto your child, and it may exacerbate the child's problems.

For example, Grant and his wife, Gina, run their family business. They were under pressure to meet a tough deadline on a project, and their anxiety in the household was high. Their kids soaked up some of that stress, and each acted out in different ways. Their son became lethargic and developed a cold virus that lingered for weeks. Their daughter started acting out in her first-grade class by hitting classmates when she got upset.

Grant and Gina were beside themselves. When they took their son to the doctor, she suggested he might have picked up a rare virus during their recent trip abroad. The doctor noted the boy's weight loss and referred them to a nutrition specialist, so Grant and Gina immediately started obsessing about every forkful that entered their son's mouth. And how could their docile daughter begin acting up at exactly the *worst* possible time, when they were already so stressed out about their son?

From our coaching sessions, Gina remembered that if their kid developed a mysterious illness or started acting up at school, it was a red flag. They figured it was because they were under pressure, and it was spreading to their kids now. They began to examine whether they had been more distant recently, perhaps avoiding unpleasant topics or decisions that they had to make. This realization didn't solve the problem of their tough project deadline, but it helped them reduce their *drama* about the deadline, and the drama about their children's symptoms, which immediately began to improve their children's well-being.

Have you ever come home tense from work and snapped at your kid? That's an obvious example of the phenomenon I'm describing here. There are a thousand subtle ways that we unknowingly spray our stress and anxiety onto our spouse and children. When somebody develops a symptom, that is a signal to consider whether the level of anxiety in the herd of your family has hit critical mass.

Have you ever wondered why problems like the above always seem to show up at the worst possible moment? The problems show up *because it is* the worst possible moment. We've already sprayed our anxiety on our kids, they begin acting out, and our already heightened anxiety leaves us primed to overreact.

How do we lower our anxiety? The first act is to notice when you're stuck in a vicious circle. As long as you're worried about your child's symptoms, you're hooked in. You're caught up in a vicious circle of escalating anxiety, because the more you focus on and worry about your child's symptoms, the worse her symptoms seem to get. This in turn worries you more, and the whole thing continues to escalate, because it's extremely difficult to cut through the emotional chaos in your head. But it would simplify your life greatly if you became aware that it might be your anxiety that is clouding your view of the situation with your child. If you can begin to at least wonder whether there's something underneath your child's symptoms, you're on the right track.

Just to be clear: I'm not saying don't go to the doctor if it's a health-related problem. I am saying we should have the symptoms treated, *and* ask ourselves "What is going on in me or my marriage that needs to be addressed?"

If you can see your kid's problems as symptoms of the level of anxiety in you or your marriage, then your perception of the problem changes. You can almost be grateful that someone is giving you a red flag. Perhaps something needs to be addressed in your marriage, or in the way you're handling a tough situation with your job or your own parents. You know you've become an enlightened master if you can almost playfully say to yourself, "Lucky me! My kid's allergic reaction has shown me it's time to talk to my spouse about our finances!"

"How can that be?" you may ask. "My kid's problem is allergies, but I don't have allergies," or "I've never had a learning disability in my life — how could I have given my kid one?" However, allergies are only a symptom. The underlying cause is anxiety. Your child likely has an increased level of anxiety, which is manifesting in the form of a symptom.

At a recent social gathering, a parent thanked me for an insight she gained from one of my seminars on this type of self-fulfilling prophecy. She said, "My son has asthma, and I realized that every time I heard him cough my anxiety would spike. It even got to the point where he was afraid to cough in front of me! Your seminar taught me how to focus on what was going on in my marriage when my son coughed. I began to notice that I overreacted to my son's cough the most when my husband and I were avoiding tough topics in our marriage, and I was anxious. But whenever I calmed down about my son's cough, his symptoms seemed to improve! So now I argue more with my husband, but my son is healthier. I don't mind making *that* trade-off!"

Does it seem far-fetched that anxiety would be a factor in your child's allergies? Most people accept that when we're stressed, it lowers our immune response. Allergies involve the body's immune response. As we discussed in chapter 1 on projection, allergies may be symptoms of high stress and anxiety levels in your child.

The best way to cure the symptom is to cure the cause. Whereas we will never be rid of anxiety, we can take steps to lower it in our children by lowering it in ourselves, and by not passing it on via projection. That benefits everyone.

Of course, to see your child's disturbing problem as a red flag in your own life is easier said than done. With practice, however, it becomes easier.

## If You Feel Guilty, Read This

I understand that some parents are feeling guilty as they read this. The idea that we somehow cause our children's suffering might seem unbearable. But our goal here is not to beat ourselves up: there was no malice on our part; we didn't even know we were doing it! Instead, the goal is to confront a painful reality now, so that both we and our kids can feel less pain in the future. Our denial regarding our kid's issues isn't helping anyone, and in the long run the problem will only be compounded, as their issues become more serious and cause us more worry. So believe me, as painful as it is, short-term pain for long-term gain is the way to go. And remember: you're not alone. We parents *all* engage in projection to some degree. We're just playing the hands we were dealt by our families of origin.

And if you begin to notice your tendency to project, your relief from worry will be immense. When a child's problem causes us great worry, we may feel powerless and afraid of the unknown. When a child's problem is viewed as a red flag about ourselves, it's almost a relief. Suddenly we have some control over the situation. There are things we can do that will make both our child and us feel better.

So we have nothing to lose by viewing our child's symptoms as red flags of anxiety in us — even if the symptoms don't improve, we'll attach less drama to the symptoms, so it still helps us cope with the situation better. It's like my wife's favorite saying. Whenever something crummy happens, she says, "That's perfect!" What she means is that the crummy event holds an opportunity to think about a challenge in a new way. We may learn something, or be motivated to change something. She believes everything happens for a reason, even if sometimes only God understands. Claiming, "That's perfect!" even when it's not perfect at that moment, helps us to reframe the drama we attach to a problem. Often in retrospect, we can see how an unfortunate occurrence actually *did* benefit us in the long term.

The mind is a powerful thing, and anxiously focusing on a symptom has the power to make it worse. Of course we would never intentionally "dump" our worry by creating a symptom in our child, but what if we're passing on our emotional baggage without realizing it?[2]

Anxiety is just anxiety until someone complains of physical pain, or gets a diagnosis from an expert. Once a symptom has been diagnosed, it can take on a reality of its own. Now we worry about the real, tangible symptom, rather than focusing on the anxiety that may have caused it. At that point, it's much harder to put the genie back in the bottle.

Michael Kerr tells the story of his counseling sessions with a schizophrenic daughter and her mother. The daughter was catatonic, and the psychiatrist told her mother she should be less controlling of her catatonic daughter if she wanted her daughter to improve (emphasis on the word "should"). The following week, the mother wrote a letter to the psychiatrist, saying that she felt "diminished" by his comment.

Now this was an interesting puzzle: The mother brought the daughter to counseling because she wanted them both to feel better. The psychiatrist gave her his best advice. He was speaking from experience, observation, and strong personal convictions; he believed that the daughter would improve if the mother was less intrusive. And yet, when he gave the mother the key to improving both her daughter's and her own well-being, the mother took offense, and could only hear the doctor's advice as blaming her for poor mothering.

The mother wanted her child to be healed, but she wasn't able to participate in the healing. This may be one of the biggest obstacles to progress for children with problems.

Their parents feel tremendous love and concern for their child. The parents secretly worry that their child's problem is somehow their fault (e.g., "If only we had showed our child more attention, or been more strict, or less strict, this all could have been avoided. . . . "). That's why parents are almost relieved when experts tell them that their child's problem is genetic, or a chemical imbalance. They are now free of guilt and blame. The mother did not want to be less intrusive, and she did not want to believe she had anything to do with the illness of her daughter.

Unfortunately, a parent's relief is only temporary, because the child's problem doesn't improve, nor does their anxiety about their child. In fact, parents would be wise to hear the bad news up front, so that they can have some good news later.

But who wants to face that reality? Our parenting instinct and our love for our children is so strong that it is crushing to imagine we have caused any harm to our flesh and blood. We can't bear to imagine we have failed our children as parents, and we'd much rather yell at a doctor than face that possibility. So let me give you the best news yet. This is far better news than, "Your child's problem is genetic or a chemical imbalance." My news is this: it's not your fault as a parent. You are not to blame, but you can benefit everyone by taking responsibility for it.

You are not to blame for your child's problem, even if you can name ways you actively contributed to it. You are not to blame even if others tell you that you were insensitive or ignorant toward your child. You are not to blame because either you didn't know what you were doing, or you knew but you couldn't help yourself. As discussed in chapter 5 on anxiety, most of us are not aware when we are anxiously passing on our emotional baggage to our children. We do it without thinking. We don't question our behavior because that's the way things are done in our family. The generations before us thought and behaved in this manner, and the power of their legacy to influence how we think and behave is much greater than we realize.

Hopefully you now agree with me that you didn't choose the cards that were dealt to you, so there's no use in blaming yourself or your hapless parents for the cards you got. They're just passing on the cards they were dealt by the herd instinct among their ancestors. As my son likes to say, "You get what you get, and you don't get upset." So what does it mean to take responsibility? Do we have to take the blame for the stuff our ancestors passed down to us?

Hardly.

### Step 4:
### Recognize More of Your Own Drama
### So That You Will Be Less Anxious and
### Thus Pass Less Baggage On to Your Child

To take responsibility means to stop blaming the dealer for your cards, and just play your hand the best you can.

In life, we waste a lot of time and energy whining at the dealer. Some of us whine at our parents for the mess they passed on to us. Some of us whine at God for the cruel fate he has handed us. Some of us whine at our boss, our spouse, our ungrateful kids, our kid's teacher or coach. We all wish we had been dealt better cards. We feel entitled to better cards than we got.

But for all the time we spend whining and moaning about our cards, our hand sits there, unplayed. The clock's ticking, and before you know it your life will be Game Over. It's crazy not to pick up your hand and start playing. You can't win if you don't play.

Who inspires us in life? I bet you it's not the people who were dealt a great hand and played it well. It's the people who were dealt a worse hand than you, and played their hands like a champ. Those are the people we want to read about and watch on TV. Those are the people we learn from. A poker player will tell you that any hand's a winner and any hand's a loser; it's all about what you do with what you've got.

Taking responsibility may sound like hard work, but it's a shortcut compared to the path you're on now. If you're like most of us, you have excellent "reasons" for why your life hasn't turned out as you had planned. You can list the people who are to blame for messing up your life. You can explain the obstacles that blocked your steps forward. You can point out the unlucky breaks and your personal weaknesses that impede your progress. Meanwhile, you're not making the progress you could. You have many other people and things to blame, you feel plenty of anger and bitterness toward them, and you suffer enormously while you curse the rut you're stuck in. Without realizing it, you've chosen the Route of Maxi-Suffering and Mini-Progress.

What we need to do instead is take responsibility for our own lives. This will remove the pressure of our anxious, hand-wringing focus on our child's perceived problem. It will also set a great example, as we create better lives for ourselves that our kids will then look up to. As Carl Jung said, "Children are educated by what the grown-up *is* and not by his talk." In the following example, one parent had to take a hard look at who he was before he could talk to his son:

When Ken picked up his kids from summer day camp, two staffers crowded around him and anxiously told of how his seven-year-old son, Andrew, had been teased almost to tears by two ten-year-old girls on a camp field trip. Ken's first reaction was anger. How dare two older kids gang up on a younger one like that! He found one of the girls and spoke to her on the spot, but the girl seemed so sullen and insolent that it was like talking to a stone. The staffers had also spoken to these girls, with little effect.

His son was sobbing that he didn't want to go back to camp anymore.

What to do? I walked Ken through three steps:

1. There's the problem, and the *drama* about the problem; separate the problem from your feelings about the problem.

2. Research your kid's problem in your family of origin; interview relatives.

3. Use any insights you gain to calm yourself about the problem; this will help you become more resourceful and able to see more options that could help solve the problem.

"Kids (and adults) get teased every day," I said to Ken. "Why does this evoke such emotion in you?" It turns out that when Ken himself was a boy, he had been singled out on the school bus and teased mercilessly. Nothing seemed to stop the teasing: he was terrified to tattle because tattling would mean being shunned by his peers.

When Ken began to research the teasing problem in his own family, it brought back a lot of memories. Ken said he could remember his father describing how all his life he'd been oversensitive. He told Ken how as a boy he had the fastest horse in their county, but he was crushed when the others would tease him that his horse was ugly. Ken remembers his dad's awkward attempts to coach him on what to do with his tormentors. Ken always felt highly uncomfortable in those conversations, and his dad's advice always seemed out-of-touch and uncool.

The worst was the time his dad secretly spoke to the parents of Ken's worst tormentor. The teasing stopped for a while, but his former tormentor told all the other kids, who had smug smirks on their faces as they whispered and giggled about "the tattletale." Ken was furious with his father for going behind his back. His father had the best of intentions, but he had made things much worse.

So you see already how this teasing problem now spans three generations? Ken never knew his father's parents, but his mother's father was famous for being touchy and overreactive. And Ken's siblings often nod knowingly behind his mother's back about how easily her feelings are hurt; it's almost like they walk on eggshells around her. Furthermore, several of Ken's siblings were severely teased as well.

What Ken found was that as he researched this issue within his family, his perceptions changed. When he found out that this problem spanned several generations, he began to feel less like there was something wrong with him. When he discovered that other relatives had fought back or run away from their bullies (with mixed results), he began to blame himself less for his inaction. And when he saw how prevalent it was in his family, Ken felt less bitter about being a victim. In a word, Ken began to put his son's problem in perspective; against the backdrop of generations of teasing in his family, it no longer seemed like such a big deal. He could view things a little more thoughtfully, which means he was managing his anxiety better: his cortex was taking over from the anxious response of his amygdala.

Beware the self-fulfilling prophecy. Most parents who were teased as children then go on to worry so much about their child's welfare that they create their own worst nightmare. They overreact, blowing things out of proportion, and unintentionally pass on their teasing legacy to their child.

The very next day, Andrew came home from camp, bursting to tell him the injustice he had suffered once again at the hands of the same two girls. But this time, Ken did something different. He sat down, turned off the phone, and took five minutes to write the facts down on paper. He asked Andrew many questions, like: "How did it start? What did she say? What was your reply? What did the other girl say? How did you respond? Did you tell a grown-up? What did they say?"

This process of getting the facts was calming to both Andrew and Ken, because it forced them to think more clearly and objectively about an emotional situation. When we're upset, we tend to focus on *why*. We try to guess, or make up reasons for, why so-and-so did these terrible things. Humans are meaning-making machines, and sometimes we assume that the motives of those who upset us are much worse than they actually were. We overreact. But asking the four W's — who, what, where, when — but never *why*, can help us to find calm, resourceful solutions to upsetting problems.

Next, Ken did something radically different from his typical response. He didn't call the teacher or drive over to the girls' houses. He leaned back in his chair, and said, "Well, people can be mean at times. Both kids *and* grown-ups can be mean. I deal with this at my office too, so I think this is a chance to learn how to deal with mean people. Andrew, how would you like to handle this?"

Silence.

Finally, Andrew replied, "I don't know." Ken responded, "Well, I can think of a few options. We could go to your camp teacher, and I'll stand beside you while you say what you want. Or we could drive over to the girls' homes, and I'll stand beside you while you say what you want, to them or to their parents. Or we can practice some funny comebacks that you can use the next time they try to upset you. If you defend yourself with humor, they might leave you alone."

At first, Andrew wanted to go talk with his teacher, but when they rehearsed what he might say, he didn't come up with much. So he and Ken decided to practice simple and funny comebacks that he could apply to any situation. For example, if someone calls him a dummy, Andrew smiles, and exclaims with mock amazement, "Oh! I didn't know you were a dummy!" If someone tells him to shut up, Andrew says with mock joy, "What a *polite* thing to say! Thank you!"

Both Ken and Andrew found themselves chuckling as they practiced his lines, and the pain of teasing had been transformed into the confidence of being able to handle himself in any situation. I hope it's clear that the lesson here is not about the exact words the child chooses. It's about self-reliance.

Ken is not rushing in to protect his child every time he faces injustice. However, he is willing to stand beside him if he chooses to speak to a teacher or a mean child.

Of course, sometimes bullies need to be handled by parents. But we parents need to calm ourselves down in order to do what's best in the long run. Teaching kids to take care of themselves prepares them for the real world. Kids can learn to look at the facts, choose their own solution, and practice it with supervision. I believe mentoring and practice are the best ways for a child to learn to take care of himself — not always intervention. We adults have no one to tattle to, so we have to work things out among ourselves. Our kids would do well to learn that lesson before adulthood.

I'm not claiming a 100 percent cure, but even a 25 percent cure will ease the size of the mountain Ken creates over his son's molehill. In a sense, the buck stops here, with him.

Because Ken was able to focus less on his fears for his son, Andrew will suffer less of the legacy that's been passed down to him. And perhaps he'll pass on less of that legacy himself. The emotion surrounding this issue is now a little smaller. Ken attaches less emotional drama to it, so it attracts less emotional drama than it used to.

## Summary:
## Avoiding the Self-Fulfilling Prophecy

Here is how to spot and avoid a self-fulfilling prophecy: First, treat any problem in your child as a symptom of a problem in yourself or your marriage. Second, notice the many subtle ways you may inadvertently create your own worst nightmare in your child. Remember that you and your child are herd animals, and anxiety is contagious; it can pass easily from you to your child. Remember the story of the woman at the party who thanked me for my seminar because she and her husband were arguing more, but her kid was coughing less. Find your child's problem within you or your marriage. As we discussed in chapter 7, research this problem in your family of origin and look for patterns.

Insight into the Big Picture of how this problem originated will calm you and give you valuable objectivity. Bring that objectivity to your child's problem: Calm yourself down by getting the facts and empower your child. Even a 25 percent cure is better, especially when you now have clarity on this process: your child's problem → your problem → getting the facts on your family of origin's problem.

When one of your kids has a problem, don't nag him, or blame your spouse, or feel guilty about it. If you can reduce your drama around problems, then it's much easier to locate the source and solve it.

While it may be uncomfortable to look at our own flaws and how they may be affecting our loved ones, this painful self-discovery is actually the shortest route to relief for you *and* your child. Facing the problem in yourself will help you pass one less piece of baggage on to your kids.

That said, we all know how hard it can be to follow through sometimes, even when we know it's for the best. In the next chapter, we'll look at what prevents us from following through with our kids and how we can make it easier to do the right thing for our children in the long run.

# Chapter Nine

# We Get So Much Good Advice, but Why Can't We Follow Through?

Cynthia was concerned. Her kids, eight and ten years old, never helped her prepare meals or clean up afterward, and their rooms were a disaster area. How would these kids grow up to raise a family and run a household of their own?

One day after school, Cynthia took a stand. On the fridge she posted a schedule listing each child as cleaning up after dinner on every other night of the week. She calmly told them, "I apologize for being irresponsible to you. You must learn to cook and clean so you can take care of yourselves when you grow up. From now on, I will not clean up for you after dinner. That is where I stand. If the kitchen isn't cleaned up to my satisfaction, you'll lose all desserts and snacks the next day." Then she hid all the junk food in the house.

Her son was first on the clean-up schedule, but he went off to watch TV. The next day he watched his sister eat candy after school while he got nothing. He used his best persuasion tactics, alternating between screaming at Cynthia and bouts of crying. To all of his tirades and attempts to negotiate, Cynthia calmly repeated one phrase: "You know what's right." That night, her daughter begrudgingly cleaned up, but did a lazy, sloppy job. The next day she went without sweets. Same protests and debates. Same response from Cynthia: "You know what's right." It took all of her courage to stay the course, but soon Cynthia had children who knew how to take care of a kitchen, and they were on their way to learning how to take care of themselves.

Cynthia was inspired by this experience. Her husband chronically used to forget to buy milk, so she would nag him or else go get it herself. One day, she told him she would no longer go get milk when he came home empty-handed. One morning, the kids came down for breakfast and asked where the milk was for their cereal. "Go ask your father," Cynthia replied. He never forgot the milk again.

So many parenting books tell us the right things to do, but why can't we follow through? We will cover these five points:

1. When we parents think we're "helping" our child, it may be our own anxiety talking: we avoid our own discomfort by caving in to our children's demands, rather than doing what's best for them in the long run.

2. Our need for approval stems from our primal herd instinct and the need to fit in. We can learn to recognize our herd instinct, which helps us to rise above our need for approval, so we can do what's right for our kids.

3. Disciplining our children begins with disciplining ourselves. Creating a new identity in our family of origin will help us grow the courage we need to give our kids the discipline they need.

4. When we break the rules of roles and relationships in our families, we can expect pressure to "change back."

5. To raise happy kids, pursue your passion and get a life yourself!

If today's households seem chaotic compared to the families we grew up in, it's because they are. The above points are crucial because we need to distinguish between what *seems* to help a child in the moment and what *actually* helps a child in the long run. Sometimes it's hard to discipline our child, but we can learn to view discipline as an act of love in terms of assuring our child's future development.

Many of us parents want to be our kids' friends, not their parents. But today's kids are not happier, despite today's more permissive parenting. Given the number of kids with serious acting out issues, common sense tells us that less discipline does not equal more fulfilled children. In this chapter, we'll learn how to follow through on what we know is right for our kids.

## "Helping" Is Actually Hurting

Many parents are trying harder to make their family life work, but they're getting worse results. In 1965, 60 percent of families had a breadwinner father and a stay-at-home mother. Today that model comprises only 30 percent of families, but amazingly, time-diary research shows that married and single parents actually spend more time teaching, playing with, and caring for their children than parents did forty years ago.[1]

Anxiety runs high in many of today's families. Parents blog at tens of thousands of sites, seeking advice on teaching compassion, empowering their kids, and raising high achievers — at the same time they worry about the scourge of perfectionism in their own lives and their kids' lives.[2]

This trend of overparenting has yielded legions of depressed mothers, sexless marriages, and children who have no boundaries. These parents believe it is noble to sacrifice everything for their children, but end up feeling more disappointed with their results rather than fulfilled. "Our refusal to let our children 'cry it out' at night and our penchant for co-sleeping [is] producing a generation of dangerously sleep-deprived mothers, plodding through life in what one study called a generalized 'state of despair,'" said Judith Warner.[3]

Our generation of overachieving parents has taken overparenting too far. The mother-infant bond plays a wonderful role in newborn and infant development, but later there comes a time for emotional weaning. The overachievers that Warner describes have begun to sense that they have given up too many boundaries, to the detriment of their children's development. In our example, before her experiment, Cynthia's kids protested so much when she asked them to do chores that she felt uncomfortable insisting, so she just let it slide. But she was left wondering how her kids would ever learn to cook and clean for themselves.

We like to think we're helping family members when we do their jobs for them. In fact, we may be selfishly giving in to our discomfort with the tension, instead of letting family members learn consequences and grow up to manage themselves. We're so desperate to be loved by our children that we sell out what's best for them in order to avoid confronting our own anxiety about their disapproval or expressions of upset. We have to take a good hard look at who we're really serving.

If you give up your boundaries and dignity to assuage your kids, they're never satisfied or grateful anyway. Give them an inch and they'll take a mile — while disdaining you for not standing up to them. Do you remember Ann from chapter 2, who gave her daughter, Nina, more and more love, but Nina felt more dissatisfied and eventually shunned her mom to hang out with a bad crowd of her peers? More love did not turn out to yield good results for Ann or her daughter.

Our kids don't need more friends. They need a parent who's not afraid to be a parent. In other words, they need parents who can notice and manage their own anxiety in the moment.

Let's return to our example to explore how Cynthia built the courage she needed to discipline her kids and to do what was best for their future. She followed the advice discussed in chapter 7 and went on safari in her family of origin.

## How to Reduce Your Worry about What Others Think of You

Cynthia had long been aware that she tended to be a people-pleaser and a rescuer who bent over backward to make sure everyone in the room was happy. When she researched this trait among her parents and siblings, she noticed how powerfully this role had been imprinted on her. Her mother had a temper, and when she got upset no one dared go near her except Cynthia. When two of her siblings started an argument at the dinner table, all heads turned expectantly to Cynthia to calm things down. She couldn't necessarily say *how* she had been shaped to take on this role, but the tacit expectations of her role in the family were loud and clear. But it was only now that she became consciously aware of it.

What drove Cynthia to be the people-pleaser and rescuer? Her high anxiety made her very sensitive to anxiety in others. She felt uncomfortable being around anyone who was upset, so she calmed them down in order to get a little relief for her own anxiety. That's why for Cynthia it felt too uncomfortable *not* to intervene when her mother's anger spilled over, and she couldn't bear to feel as if she had let her family down by not calming any squabble that broke out. She unconsciously played the role her family had unconsciously assigned to her. Her desire to fit in was a powerful force within her — as it is in all of us.

We humans are hard-wired to worry about what other people think of us, because this instinct is essential to our survival. Humans, like most primates and mammals, are herd animals. Our herds are called families, but we also join other herds, like corporations, teams, churches, PTOs, and service clubs. And our reputation matters in these groups. We all worry about what other people think; sometimes we just don't like to admit it.

The Japanese have a saying, "The nail that sticks out gets hammered down." In the herds of families or corporations, we know that if we make too many waves, we risk ostracism and isolation. We crave the approval of fitting in, and yet we yearn to stand up for what we believe in. We find it hard to stop playing the stilted role our families handed down to us, because that would make us stick out in our families.

Most of us feel within ourselves that tug of war between wanting to fit in and yearning to follow our own heart: the struggle between individuality and togetherness. We don't read books and watch movies about people who are popular conformists; we love the drama of the person who stands up for what he believes in, whatever the cost. Many of us yearn to emulate the great leaders, from Jesus to Gandhi to Martin Luther King, who had the courage to speak the truth and to rally the minority despite the ire of the authorities.

So why don't more of us stand up for what we believe in? Quite simply, we're afraid of being disliked, so we go along with the pull of the group.

But if you and I ever hope to make a difference in this world (or in our families), it requires that we rise above the pack. We can train ourselves to do so by defining ourselves within our families: our principles, beliefs, and what we will and will not do. When we can calmly stand up for principles and beliefs in the face of family pressure, then we begin to conquer our fear of disapproval. We can do what's best for our marriages and children in the long run, rather than just caving in to our anxiety in the moment. Our home lives can go from chaos to calm. Our kids can learn how to be citizens rather than consumers — and they're actually happier for it.

How can we get the courage we need to stand up for what we believe in?

The answer can be found in our own herd, our family of origin. If we can begin to overcome the herd instinct in our own family of origin, we will no longer be held hostage by our need to fit in.

Like the offspring of all other mammals, human offspring are subject to imprinting. As discussed in chapter 5, imprinting is a fancy word for how our families "train" us to play certain roles in our families. Cynthia had already identified her role as the people-pleaser/rescuer, and next she learned how to monitor and control her anxiety while standing right in the middle of the chaos of her family of origin. She took a crash course in her family's history, so neither she, nor her children, would have to repeat it. Let's explore a detailed, real-life example of Cynthia discovering how much her family's herd instinct influenced her behavior. Then we'll study how stepping outside of her old role empowered her to stand up for what she knew was right for her children.

## Playing Detective and Solving Family Mysteries

Cynthia's mother has always had a keen interest in genealogy, but, strangely, Cynthia's mother always studied Cynthia's father's ancestors and not her own family of origin. The story among Cynthia's siblings was that Mom came from a small family on her side and had very few relatives. They all accepted this, and it never even occurred to them to question it.

But one day Cynthia broke the unwritten rules of her family.

With the help of two genealogy experts, Cynthia had begun to research the ancestry of her mother. Her discoveries led her back hundreds of years, but the search also spread out to discover many cousins as well. To Cynthia's surprise, it turned out that her mother has over 150 living relatives in the United States and Canada, as well as England, France,

Cyprus, and Australia. Her mom wasn't from a small family, but she was from a family cloaked in secrecy.

Cynthia's biggest discovery was that her maternal grandfather, Noah, had abandoned his first wife, as well as their three daughters. Her grandpa came home from World War I to find his wife holding a baby boy that obviously wasn't his. He turned around and walked out the door and never returned — abandoning three daughters of his own blood. He traveled to a neighboring state and then met and moved in with Cynthia's grandma. Noah and Cynthia's grandmother both went to their graves claiming that they were husband and wife, since to live together without being married was considered scandalous back then in their community.

What nobody in Cynthia's family knew was that her mother had three half-sisters — those three daughters her grandpa abandoned, who had gone on to marry and have many children of their own. Her half-sisters were dead before Cynthia's mom could meet them, but some of her mom's nieces and nephews were living only forty-five minutes away from her.

Discovering many missing branches of her family tree was just one of Cynthia's adventures as she went on the kind of safari we discussed in chapter 7. Bringing her family's hidden past into the light helped her see her family in a whole new way. Discovering the full portrait of her family's history gave her the courage and insight to redraw her own image within that portrait.

However, as she would soon discover, her family didn't want her to change. She would first have to run the gauntlet of her family's herd instinct, which pressured her to conform to her old role. It all began when she broke the unwritten code of conduct in her family.

## Reunion: Bringing the Demons Out of the Closet

Cynthia had been speaking to all these newfound relatives in the course of her research and had developed fledgling relationships with them. So she offered to organize a family reunion so that they could all come together and get in touch with their roots. Her mom's response was a luke-warm green light.

Cynthia's siblings' response was something else. Her eldest sister had organized a couple of previous reunions on their dad's side of the family. But she knew almost none of their mom's relatives, so she agreed to do this one together with Cynthia.

But almost immediately, strange things began to happen.

They had planned a full weekend of activities in a beautiful city with a good airport. Since many folks were coming from thousands of miles away, Cynthia wanted to plan a weekend full of activities to make the trip worth their while. Then she got a cryptic e-mail from her sister, saying that they were only going to have a one-day reunion on a Saturday. Cynthia reluctantly agreed. The sister wrote again a week later, saying that the reunion would only be from noon to 6:00 p.m., since the elderly relatives would tire easily. She implied that their whole family agreed with her, including their mom.

Cynthia was mystified. Why would their relatives bother to fly or drive thousands of miles for a six-hour get-together? And if her mom and siblings didn't want to attend a whole weekend of activities, they could simply not show up. Why did they care whether the rest of the relatives got together or not?

That's when Cynthia broke some more rules. She told her sister that if their mom and siblings didn't want to attend, she was fine with that but she was going to go ahead and organize a whole weekend anyway.

And that's when all hell broke loose.

Cynthia's mom happened to be visiting her at the time, and they called Cynthia's sister on speaker phone. Then both her mother and sister screamed at Cynthia with a level of emotion that was far out of proportion to her alleged crime. Cynthia's brother left her answering machine messages full of curses. Another sister told Cynthia she couldn't stay with her during the reunion or use her car, and then she booked a ticket to California so she wouldn't be around for the reunion. And her eldest sister sent out a revised invitation to all these relatives she didn't even know, contradicting Cynthia's initial invitation to come for the whole weekend. Cynthia looked hard for logical reasons for this bomb blast of emotion in her family, but could find none. Why all the drama?

When one family member changes her role and relationships in the family, it has a ripple effect through everyone else's role and relationships in the family. This causes extreme anxiety and upheaval in the family. It's not about logic. It's about the herd instinct. Cynthia's herd had trained each other how to function together in the herd, and they had functioned that way for decades: Cynthia's job was to smooth things out — not to stir things up! Moreover, Cynthia's family had been trained that Mom had no relatives. They didn't know or ask about Mom's relatives and they certainly didn't meet with them. They had been trained that their oldest sister ran all family get-togethers, and that was the way things had always been. But most importantly, the dynamic of Cynthia's herd was about to be affected by dozens of "new" members to the herd that they never knew existed. Cynthia's herd was extremely nervous about this new chaos and went into extreme emotional upheaval.

Fortunately, Cynthia realized that if she was going to change her role and way of interacting with her family, she could expect intense pressure to "change back" — that is to say, to act the way she had always acted in the family — as the people pleaser and peacemaker. The way you can tell whether your family is staging a change-back is that each member attacks you personally, with all the cajoling, threats, gossip, and venom they can muster. They will give reasons that make no logical sense for why you've made a monumental mistake. Then, if you hold your course and don't return fire, they will calm down and act as if they were never rude to you.[4]

Clearly, Cynthia had changed the family dynamic, and she was experiencing a change-back. At times she felt so anxious, hurt, and isolated that she wanted to give up. Cynthia felt terrible to be disliked and criticized. She likes to fit in and feel she's a part of her herd, winning other members' approval and praise. But it had become too costly to fit in. Cynthia knew that if she wanted to make anything of her life, she had to learn how to be herself in her family, without them running her life. She had to find a way to be an individual within the herd, rather than a conforming sheep.

So while inwardly terrified, Cynthia held her ground. She held the reunion over a full weekend, and many people flew in two days early to meet and greet the family members they never knew they had. Cynthia's family calmed down, and everyone attended except the sister who left for California. They had a good time, and her family acted almost as if nothing had ever happened.

## The Pay-Off

The greatest gift the reunion gave Cynthia was that she learned to hear her own inner voice. Whereas in the past she had unconsciously let others define who she is, Cynthia began to define herself. She got much greater clarity about who she was, what she believes, what matters to her, and what she will (or will not) do. As Cynthia got clearer, she got calmer, so she didn't feel compelled to counterattack or justify her every move to her family. She stayed in close contact with each member. Her goal was not to change their minds or to get her way. She was simply getting clear on the things she was willing to do, and the things she was *not* willing to do. She showed them she still loved them, but she related to them more as someone who thinks for herself.

True maturity and independence is to notice and control your anxiety while staying in close contact with your family. Defining yourself anew in your family causes emotional upheaval in your herd at first, but eventually the herd may even come to see you as a leader in their midst. There's a difference between being a rebel and growing a backbone.

Cynthia was no longer held hostage to her family by her need for their approval. She no longer felt so pressured to please them, or go along with what the group wanted her to do. She could withstand more of their criticism, gossip, and shunning. She could say and do what she believed in more calmly and more firmly. And it was only after she cared less about what they thought about her that Cynthia became aware of just how obsessed she had been with her family's approval. Cynthia was finally growing up.

Now, with Cynthia's story in mind, let's return to the question, "If so many parenting books give us good advice, why don't we follow through?" I think one of the things that prevents us from following through is our herd instinct — our need to follow the pull of the group, and play our assigned role. If we cave in to our fear of upsetting our loved ones, our family often caters to the loudest voice, rather than the best principles. We have to learn how to take a stand in our families of origin in order to take a stand with spouse and children.

Cynthia's research and reunion project with her parents and siblings helped her to recognize the role she played in her family, to step outside of it, and to withstand her family's pressure on her to change back. This new behavior helped her create a more constructive role for herself, even under pressure. Once she was more herself in her family of origin, she was able to see the influence of anxiety and herd instinct on her parenting. And her newfound courage allowed her to take a stand with her own two children and set up the discipline that would serve them well in the long run.

Your role in your family of origin may differ from Cynthia's, but the strategy is the same. The goal is to go on safari and get some awareness of your role and then see if you can think for yourself while acting in your family. This is hard, lifelong work, and the temptation is always to try to change other family members. But there is relief in discovering that you can't change your parents or siblings — it's a dead end — so you only have to focus on changing yourself, which is much easier.

Let's return to the question, If we all want happy, well-behaved kids, then why don't we enforce boundaries? Because the parent who can't enforce boundaries may not *have* a boundary between herself and her child. She may be oversensitive to their attunement, such that she feels her child's upset so strongly in *her* body that she cannot help but intervene to soothe him, in order to get some relief.

Cynthia's example, with her safari in her family of origin, shows how our goal is about more awareness of our own herd instincts and anxiety and training ourselves not to act from them. You might say this is how parents can "grow themselves up," in a way. As we saw in chapters 7 and 8, this involves taking responsibility for our anxiety and doing work on our relationships with our family of origin. It's perfectly okay to be anxious. We just don't want to *act* from it. We need to be able to separate ourselves from our child's upset. We need boundaries.

We will next examine four parenting examples that show that, in many ways, parenting is about disciplining ourselves: managing our anxiety so we can make the right decision for the long-term good of the family. Below are four examples of families who created boundaries that made their households a pleasure.

## Example #1:
## Accidentally Training Your Kid for Life

Vic and Kendra didn't realize it at the time, but they did something that changed their entire parenting experience for life. They had heard about a strategy of short-term pain for long-term gain, which they called "Five-Ten-Fifteen." One Friday night six months after their first child, Connor, was born, they decided to train him to go to sleep at a specific bedtime. They laid him in his crib at 9:00 p.m., turned out the light, left the door ajar, and started their stop watch.[5]

Connor started to cry. His plaintive wails tore at his parents' heart strings, but they waited a full five minutes before they went into the room. Both Vic and Kendra spoke gently and lovingly to soothe him, but they didn't pick him up.

Connor continued to cry. In anticipation of how difficult this Friday evening would be, they had rented a video and sat down to watch it. "Like a fool, I had chosen a tense thriller of a horror movie," Vic later remarked, laughing. "With our nerves already frayed by our son's primal wails, the movie hit us like a jackhammer. Things can get crazy when you're sleep-deprived. We started imagining that the monster on the screen might actually be in our kitchen!"

When the stop watch beeped after ten minutes, they found the courage to creep past the Kitchen Monster and into Connor's room. Same drill. They spoke soothingly for thirty seconds, didn't pick him up, and left again.

This time, he didn't even slow down from his wails. "He was red-faced and looked at us like we were the cruelest parents to ever walk the planet," Kendra remembers. "We skulked out of his nursery, but we held firm."

Connor persisted through another fifteen minutes and another visit to his room, but then exhausted, he fell asleep. Kendra reports, "We were ready to check into an insane asylum, and I nearly killed Vic for renting a horror flick, but we survived."

The next night was almost the same nightmarish routine again.

And then, it was over.

The third night, Connor cried for maybe five minutes, and then went to sleep. And they don't remember what happened on the following evenings, because they had adjusted to the routine. He might whimper a tad, but then he'd play quietly in his crib for a while before drifting off to sleep.

Imagine their relief at this new routine. Now they could count on preserving their marriage, with some intimacy time and "grown-up talk" to sustain them each evening, after their child went to sleep. They could also get as much as six solid hours of slumber, to preserve their sanity so that they could parent Connor better in the long run.

But most of all, imagine Vic and Kendra's subsequent confidence. They had fought the "Dragon of Discipline," and won. Now they knew that if they could ignore their own suffering and doubt, they could withstand Connor's demands. If they persisted in doing what was right for their child in the long run, they could create positive habits that would serve the whole family.

Kendra looks back with pride on what they accomplished: "For those first few evenings, it seemed as though we stared at an insurmountable brick wall before us. When we persisted forward with our plan, we found, to our delight, that the brick wall was just an illusion — a veil through which we had passed. And on the other side of that illusory brick wall that had seemed so real, we found peace, sleep, and the confidence to train our child with good habits. That 5–10–15 has served our marriage and his development as an independent child and a future responsible member of our family and the community."

Kendra observes, "If my kids complain, I have to stop myself from doing whatever it takes to calm them down. In the moment, I find it easier to give in than to tolerate my kid's upset. I guess you could say I find it too upsetting to be with him upset."

Once a child is old enough to know better, if she creates drama, it's not helpful to soothe her. It's not compassionate to calm her down. That just makes *us* feel better. When our kid is suffering, we feel tremendous discomfort, and the fastest way to feel better is to soothe our child. Soothing her makes us feel better in the moment, but in the long run, our child has lost another opportunity to learn how to regulate herself. Nothing is more vital to a child's long-term happiness than the ability to self-regulate — to get over upsets quickly. Upsets are inevitable in life, so it's the people who can get over them who go on to succeed.[6]

## Example #2:
## Tyler and Val Write the "Family Law"

Tyler and his wife, Val, have found a way to reduce the number of anxious decision-making moments with their kids. They wrote a "Family Law" and placed it on their fridge door. It outlines which child helps prepare dinner and which child cleans up each evening. It lists the consequences if the children forget to say please or thank you, or to make their bed, or to put away their coat and backpack and wash their hands with soap when they come home from school. The consequences are not particularly severe, but they are *consistent,* so each child is clear and the parents don't have to make a tough, emotional decision in the moment. They're just enforcing the law. This makes it a lot easier to maintain boundaries.

I still remember the words of a child psychologist who said, "Children are like dogs; either you train them, or they train you." Ten or twenty years from now, I believe we'll look back and shake our heads at how we could have dreamed that parenting was as simple as "the more attention and freedom you give your kids, the better they'll turn out."

## Example #3:
## Doug and Leanne Make Mealtime a Pleasure

Doug and Leanne have learned how to set and maintain boundaries with their kids, and everyone's a winner because of it. I would describe their approach as "calm but firm." They confess they don't always live up to the "calm" part; sometimes they raise their voices in anger. But they stick to the "firm" part often enough that the kids respect both them and the rules.

Their meals at home have boundaries. They enjoy a variety of foods because Doug and Leanne made them (yes, made them) try everything on their plate. They do not cook custom meals for their kids; they eat what their parents eat. Their kids set the table, and after dinner they ask, "May I be excused?" before they clear the table and stack the dishwasher. If they claim they can't finish dinner because they have a stomachache, Doug takes them seriously: "We tell them, 'If you're sick then you have to go to bed and sleep, without any dessert or playing. Are you sure you want to do that?' Sometimes their illness is real. Most of the time they miraculously heal themselves, rather than risk losing dessert."

People frequently remark on how polite Doug and Leanne's kids are. They say please and thank you almost always, because their parents trained them with their own, homemade game show, known as "Auto-Time-Outs." Leanne says they imitate a game show with the rule that, if the children forget a please or thank you, they automatically receive an instant time-out with no warnings. For example, Doug will exclaim in a smarmy game-show host's voice, "Congratulations! You've just won a time-out!" Then they send them to a corner for about thirty seconds. The kids took up the game, and competed with each other to see who could get the fewest time-outs. After a few days, politeness was almost second-nature to them (although they still slip occasionally). Doug explained to the kids their guiding principle in training them, "People will be much more helpful to you if you are polite to them, so politeness is good for everybody." The kids understood that, because it appealed to their self-interest.

◆ ◆ ◆

If every episode of those reality-based Nanny programs on TV makes you wince, take heart. You're doing your family a favor if you can overcome your doubts and fears about introducing structure and boundaries into the lives of your children. An investment in calm-but-firm boundaries now can transform your home life from chaos to calm, and your kids will be a pleasure to be around, both now as kids and later as spouses, colleagues, or leaders in the community. Your kids can learn how to be responsible members of the community, rather than self-centered consumers — and they'll actually be happier for it!

Our kids need to learn that there are boundaries in life, and there are consequences for every choice we make (or choose not to make). As we stand up to our kids, we're also maturing in our ability to stick to principles, even in the face of pouty lips or an emotional firestorm. Not bad training for life among grown-ups, either!

Many parents tell me they would never force their child to do an activity he or she didn't like. I acknowledge that my views may be counterculture, but I believe a child is too young to know what's best for her in the long run.

I am reminded of how much I hated practicing piano when I was young.

My mother set a great example for me in parenting. She used to sell fresh eggs from our farm to raise the money for her kids' piano lessons. I hated to practice and used to complain daily. She insisted, saying, "I worked hard for those lessons, and you're darn-well going to learn music!" I resisted, but I had no choice.

I tell you the following story not to brag, but to show you what a gift my mother gave to me. In high school, I became the president of the school choir. I spent my junior year of college in Paris, where making French friends is famously difficult. But I was the only foreign male admitted to the choir of the Sorbonne, where I easily made friends because we shared a common passion for music. And in my senior year of college, I was selected to join an *a cappella* singing group that toured across America and to thirty-three countries around the world.

So is this farm boy grateful that his mother insisted he continue with his lessons? You bet. And so was Tommy, as you'll read below.

## Example #4:
## Jim "Forces" Tommy to Love Winter Sports

"I'm not going out there again, and you can't make me!" Jim's six-year-old son, Tommy, and he were standing beside an indoor ice rink. It was the afternoon free-skate time, and several sets of parents were pulling or pushing their children around the rink as music wafted over the PA system.

Jim was frustrated and despairing. He had just circled the rink twice, watching his son slip, stumble, and fall hard on his backside so many times it made Jim wince. This was Tommy's first encounter with ice. Bambi may have looked cute when stumbling around on wobbly legs, but as Jim watched his son's legs fly out from under him over and over, it was excruciating. Tommy was not having fun, Jim was absolutely miserable, and the question on both their minds was, "Why bother, if he's not enjoying it?"

Then, for a brief moment, the thinking portion of Jim's mind peeked through the storm clouds of his emotions, and he thought to himself, "There's still forty-five minutes left before public skating ends. You have nothing to lose by persisting. If he still hates it, you'll never have to come back again."

"Tommy, you *will* go out there again, or I will give you time-out and you won't have any snack. I give you my word."

His voice was hard-edged, and Tommy knew his dad meant business. Jim tried to appear firm, but inside, he was shaking like a leaf with self-doubt. Most parents would have relented at this point. Jim wondered to himself, "Am I just being mean and forcing my will upon my poor son?"

"Okay, Dad, I'll go, but just to the other side and back — and that's it!" Tommy stepped gingerly back out onto the ice, fell to one knee, and got up. Suddenly the whining and drama from before seemed to drop away, and he struggled along the blue line, slipping many times. But when he touched the other side, he looked up at Jim and said, "Dad, I did it!" Jim promised him two Gummy Bears for every time he crossed the rink. Forty-five minutes later, he had twenty-two Gummy Bears under his belt, and asked his dad to let him skate alone because Jim was slowing him down. Tommy was absolutely beaming the first time he made it around the rink without falling.

Persistence pays off.

Jim was elated. It was as if the sun had peeked through the clouds, and the storm that he thought would never end was now behind him. He had felt wretched as he watched his son's misery, but now he was proud that his persistence had paid off. Jim and his son had crossed an "emotional river" together, but they didn't give up when the current threatened to overwhelm them midstream.

The most valuable lesson Jim learned as a parent was to persist, even in the face of the drama his child created. Tommy soon learned to skate, to ski, and even to relish practicing piano with Jim, as they prepared for his weekly lessons. Tommy now loves all three activities, which he would have abandoned long ago without Jim's firm persistence.

## What True Compassion Means

Our goal as parents is to do what's best for our kids in the long run — instead of seeking the affection that feels good for a fleeting moment but leaves both you and your kids empty later. Doing what's best in the long run teaches self-reliance and respect to everyone in the family. You're doing your family a favor to introduce calm-but-firm boundaries now, so your kids can grow up to be great spouses, colleagues, and leaders in the community. That's win–win for you, your family, and for our society's future.

Here's the key question to ask yourself when making a decision on how to discipline your child: "What will this look like when she's thirteen? Or eighteen? Or twenty-one?"

How will the decisions we make now impact her when she's a teenager? When we let a transgression go because we're tired, and it's no big deal anyway, we're thinking only in the moment — not about our child's future. Every day we parents face a dozen "slippery slopes." If we let a boundary slip and default to what's easiest for now, we start to slide down that slope, and it only gets harder to get back to that original boundary. Yes, it *does* matter that she didn't say please just now. Yes, it *does* matter that she just talked sassy to you. It's a kid's job to constantly test and challenge you. It's your job to stay calm but firm.

Firmness is true love. When we want to be our child's friend, that may be good for us in the moment but bad for our kid in the future. It's fine to be your child's buddy when you're having fun together, but when she pitches a fit about how her hair's done or a blouse she doesn't like, it's not time to calm her down by indulging her. So how do we increase our firmness?

First, we need to learn to notice and control our anxiety when we're with our family of origin. We also need to get clear on the type of marriage, parenting, and life we envision for ourselves. Here's how to begin that process.

## Writing Out What You Believe

Your thorough, thoughtful answers to three questions can help you get clear on your priorities in life:

1. What do you believe about marriage and parenting, and why?
2. What principles do you live by, and why?
3. What (besides your kids) are you willing to dedicate your life to?

Once you get clear on what you stand for, you'll approach life with more certainty. Conviction is a strange paradox, in that the more you're okay with your decisions, the more people around you will tend to be okay too. Clarifying your beliefs means you can make your contribution to the world with passion, and Thomas Friedman writes correctly in *The World Is Flat* that our kids need to develop their passions more than their résumé. If we parents stop micromanaging our kids and focus instead on our passions, we'll set a great example for contributing to society and showing our kids how to develop their own mission in life. That's win–win, because it guarantees us all a fulfilling future.

## Want Happy Kids? Get a Life Yourself!

We parents need to get a life. No kidding! It's the best thing we can do to assure our kids' success. If we're pursuing a career, or volunteer work, or hobbies we love, it brings us confidence and fulfillment. Thus, we'll be less predisposed to trying to prove our value through our children's exploits.

You've heard the expression "living vicariously through our kids." We do it all the time as parents. We expect our children will be skilled at the things we do well. We hope to develop our kids in areas where we wish we had talent. That in itself isn't such a big deal. It's human nature, and I don't think we'll "cure" that tendency any time soon.

What does matter is the degree of anxiety we attach to our expectations. It may matter too much to us, for example, how our kids are doing in school. If we try to pretend it doesn't, we may be lying to ourselves. Our kids can sense how worried and intense we are about their performance, even if we say all the right words to prop them up. We ourselves may not even be aware how anxious we are about our kids' success. We think it's noble to make the sacrifices we do for our kids.

The problem is that we spend most of our energy in places where it doesn't make a difference. We try to criticize and correct our spouses and children, while ignoring things we can control.

When we get a life, our kids will too, because we'll finally leave them alone. Instead of breathing down their necks and pressuring or cajoling them in all kinds of ways that *we* think are subtle, we'll finally give our kids some breathing room. When they have some space of their own, they may be able to take a deep breath, look around themselves, and find things that really matter to them, things they really want to pursue.

I know what you're thinking: "If I get off my kid's back, he'll drown in TV, become obsessed with video games, or start a rock band!"

I've got news for you. You don't have a choice. You only think you do.

Here's a question for those of you who are working hard to help your kids succeed: Are you getting results? Are your kids taking off, and becoming smarter and more independent each day? Or does it feel like you're fighting harder just to stop them sliding lower on the academic ladder? For all the effort you're putting in, you'd think you'd see better results, right?

Maybe your child's already sinking, but you're part of the problem rather than the solution. Maybe he has to sink and to feel the sting of some real-life consequences before he can begin to take care of himself. How long can you prop him up? Through college? Just a "few extra years" in his twenties, until he gets on his feet?

And who are you really helping? Your child, or your own anxiety about your unfulfilled life and your insecurity as a parent? We have to take a good hard look at who we're really serving. We need to ask ourselves if we're doing what's best for our kids. We parents need to develop a list of our own beliefs about what is important for our families and then stick to those principles, even in the face of anxiety, resistance, and drama.

Because ultimately, it doesn't matter so much what your kids do for a living. It matters that they can provide for themselves independently, raise a family, and be responsible members of society. *That's* what matters. Every hour you spend "helping" them with their homework is time lost toward the goal of their independence. This is about setting tough boundaries regarding what you *don't* want your kids doing. At the same time, give them more space to do what *they* want to be doing — within constructive parameters of course.

So getting a life of your own not only gives you a life; it allows your kids the room they need to get a life of their own. With independence. And passion.

I'm not talking about distancing from your spouse or kids. I'm not suggesting that you go from one extreme of over-involvement with your kids to the other extreme of ignoring them and marrying your career. The trick is to find a balance. As you pursue your own independence with passion, you've set the world's greatest example for your kids.

Are you beginning to see what good news this is? You can get a life while letting your kid get a life, and you're all the better for it. Everybody wins.

## Message to Working Mothers:
## You Go, Girl!

It's not about how much time you spend with your kids; it's how you're being with them during your time together. There is nothing wrong with both parents working full time. In fact, you're setting a great example of a parent who pursues his or her own career with passion. What *is* a problem is how guilty you feel about it. You're not likely to notice just how often you feel as though you're somehow selfish, or short-changing your child. And there are plenty of messages from family, friends, and society to suggest that what you're doing is selfish. The point is that it's not the number of hours we spend with our children that determines how well they turn out; it's how we're *being* with them during that time together.

We humans are exquisitely sensitive to each other and to the signals we're constantly giving off. Any parent knows that, thanks to attunement, children can instantly smell doubt or waffling, and they immediately jump on it and start working it to their advantage. That's nothing bad on their part. The more unsure we are of ourselves around our children, the more they're going to leverage that to their advantage.

And guilt is no exception. If you worry that you're short-changing your child by working, guess what? Your child is going to feel short-changed and communicate to you in a hundred subtle ways that he in fact *is* being short-changed. This in turn will contribute to your feeling even more guilty, and so on in a downward spiral. Perhaps you'll quit your job, spend more time with your children, but then marvel in surprise that they don't seem happier or more successful. Perhaps they seem even more sullen than before. You don't have to give your kids so much attention; both you *and* they will be happier if you don't.

It stands to reason that people pursuing their passion have less time and energy to squabble with their spouse or obsess about their kids. After a strong marriage, the greatest gift you can give yourself and your children is to define yourself and what you stand for in life. Once you're clear on what you stand for, it reduces your anxiety in those decision-making moments. You'll be more effective in attaining your goals because your priorities are clear, and you feel a stronger sense of conviction and clarity.

We can make a contribution to society when we feel less compelled to fit in and be liked by everyone. When we are no longer held hostage to the approval or criticism of others,

I believe that's when we can truly change the world, both in the workplace and at home.

In sum, to discipline our children we must discipline ourselves. Our safari work can help us get clear on the role that was unconsciously assigned to us in our family of origin. Then, we can create a better role for ourselves and grow new courage by withstanding our family's pressure to change back. And we can bring that new courage to disciplining our kids more consistently. That's win–win for every family member.

In chapter 10, we'll look at how to put your marriage first.

# Chapter Ten

# Eat, Walk, and Talk Your Way to a Happier Family

My marriage received one of its greatest gifts on Anna Maria Island in Florida. We were visiting our good friends Bill and Nell Martin there, staying in their guest cottage on the beach with our two toddlers. When it was bedtime for the kids our friend handed us two walkie-talkies, and said, "Enjoy the beach!"

Once the kids were fast asleep, we turned on these technical marvels, flipped on the "voice-activated" switch, and set one walkie-talkie between the kids, like a high-tech baby monitor. We carried the other walkie-talkie with us and walked a hundred yards to the beach, with the warm water lapping at our feet as we sat on a bench. It was perfect freedom: we could hear if a kid coughed or the phone rang, so our minds were at peace. But the kids couldn't hear us unless we pushed the Talk button, so we had complete privacy. While our kids were dreaming, Karen and I had the warm surf and each other to enjoy. It was the best of both worlds: a happy parenting and fulfilling marriage moment.

Those walkie-talkies gave birth to a tradition that has transformed our family. As the kids got older, every night we would put them to bed and then walk around our yard, staying within a twenty-second sprint from the kids. Every night we looked forward to the exercise, fresh air, and the chance to unwind and share what we were thinking, feeling, and dreaming that day. No other single tradition has boosted our marriage like that thirty minutes every evening. We have Gore-Tex to brave all kinds of weather, and neither of us would dream of missing that time together.

How does one stay happily married while raising happy kids? The greatest gift you can give your children is to have a fulfilling marriage yourself, and this chapter explores three ways to do that:

1. Walk and Talk: A daily walk with your spouse works wonders for both your body and soul. Sharing your thoughts, feelings, and dreams with your spouse is your ticket to a dependable friendship that will last a lifetime.

2. Eat: At mealtimes, your family members will fall in love with a simple game, where they share the highlights and "lowlights" of their day.

3. The Shortcut to Marital Bliss — Visit Your Parents: What we resist persists. Learning to observe our own dynamics with our parents means we'll be less judgmental and more objective about ourselves, our spouses, and our children.

This material is crucial because we parents today are too quick to sacrifice our lives and our marriages for our kids. This chapter gives us practical steps to make our marriage a priority above our kids, which is win–win for the whole family.

Most of us have created child-centered families, where our children hold priority over our time, energy, and attention. But as we break our backs for our kids, our marriage and self-fulfillment go out the window while our kids become more demanding and dissatisfied. Our sacrifices may be well-intentioned, but we're actually bankrupting our families over the long run.

If children grow up seeing parents who nurture a dependable friendship and manage conflict clearly and directly, that's a great model for their future marriages. If parents put their marriage first and their children see that the world doesn't revolve around them, we're actually giving our kids better future relationships with their co-workers, bosses, and spouses.

Be best friends with your spouse, so you can be a parent to your child. As we saw in chapter 9, your child needs a parent more than a friend. And she needs her parents to have a marriage more than she needs to be the center of attention. So how does one build a dependable friendship that will last a lifetime? Here's a tip.

## Creating a Lifelong Friendship with Your Spouse

The highlight of the day for my wife and me is our evening walk. It's great because we kill two birds with one stone: we get some exercise while we also build our friendship.

Every night we can enjoy thirty minutes of exercise, fresh air, and the chance to share what we're thinking, feeling, and dreaming. Some people may be afraid to leave the kids sleeping, but we can probably hear more through a walkie-talkie than if we were watching TV downstairs.

Sharing one's thoughts, feelings, hopes, and dreams is what forms the basis of an intimate marriage.[1] Usually, one of us will start off the conversation with a problem or challenge that's on our minds and is causing us plenty of feelings. Perhaps it's one that hasn't been resolved, and we'd like to examine it with the benefit of our partner's fresh perspective and insight. It's a great opportunity to take stock of the day and look at what worked for us, what didn't, and what we'd like to try next time.

We find that in the process of articulating our murky, muddy feelings about something that's bothering us even though we're not sure why, it really brings our mind into greater clarity. When we express those worried conversations that swirl around in our heads, we can begin to engage our cerebral cortexes and to think more clearly about what before was just a jumble of amorphous, uneasy feelings. It's as if we elevate the "primal swamp" of our reptile brains to the shiny, clear computers of our cerebral cortexes and create something useful in the process.

Even arguing is more fun when you're walking! Fighting while walking makes it easier to handle those intense emotions while you're in motion: swinging our arms and legs seems to take some of the edge off the argument. And we find that it's tough to stay mad in the fresh air with all that greenery around us.

Discussing our hopes, dreams, or fantasies also helps us identify our passion in life. What starts out as amorphous ramblings can take on a life of its own when we bounce it back and forth between our minds. Many great goals and plans have taken shape on these routine little walks around the yard. It's as if you permit each other to dream big and to ramble on until things take enough shape to hit critical mass and become a vision. When you see more clearly where you want to go in life, that's half the battle to realizing those dreams.

Another favorite question of ours is: "What struck you today?" This question gives us a chance to review the day and describe any particular insights we had when we were talking with someone, reading something, or reminded of a memory by some random event. I remember telling my wife how I had cold-called a man I wanted to work with on a creative project. I had been hesitant to even pick up the phone because he was quite powerful and well known. I had almost talked myself into defeat before I picked up the phone. But when I got him on the line, it came out in our conversation that I was an Episcopal minister, and he was an elder on the board of his Episcopal church. He seemed almost more interested in that than the details of my project, and we were soon working together.

The question "What struck you?" is mostly about insight: poignant, powerful moments when we realized something. We have them every day, but we seldom hold them up to admire them or to think them through later. These are exciting moments in life, however, and they deserve center stage every day when you're sharing your life with your partner.

Likewise when you share your "enjoyment moments" of the day. Enjoyment moments are when you recapture and remember the great little moments of the day. These can be the simplest things, like the pride I felt when my son scored a goal on the soccer field, or the daily pleasure I take in brushing my daughter's hair and tying her ponytail in the morning. Relating your daily enjoyment moments to your spouse really gives your partner a snapshot of the best of each day and allows you to relive those moments of joy as well.

To be honest, you may have to force yourself a few times until this time spent together becomes routine. Sometimes it feels easier and more comfortable to distance from one another because of the feelings we each have. As we explored in earlier chapters, our own individual level of anxiety gives us many "easily pushed buttons," so it's tempting to go to our "separate corners" in life. But my wife and I find the routine of these walks helps us to transcend our "feeling mode" and distinguish our anxiety from our relationship. In other words, we are able to share more of what is going on in us without pinning the blame on our spouse for our feelings. Developing a routine is also an excellent way to fight the temptation to distance from each other.

Putting our spouse first is win–win for everyone in the family. The more you invest in your marriage, the less time you'll spend "putting out fires" with your kids. If you make your marriage your top priority, you will automatically raise happier kids. Building a dependable friendship with your spouse takes the pressure off your kids because they don't have to become your surrogate friend in an unhealthy codependence. It also sets a great example for them to emulate when they marry and start families.

Couples who claim they don't have time for each other may be in denial. They don't have time for each other because they haven't made it a priority. And it can be confrontational to take responsibility for the distancing.

## Bringing Life to Mealtimes

At mealtimes my wife and I talk about one highlight and one "lowlight" of our day. The idea is to capture a moment in time. For example, my wife could say, "I enjoyed my bike ride into work." But if she focuses on one split-second in time, she might say, "I was riding to work when the trail curved and a lovely oak in all its fall colors came into view. Seeing that natural beauty give me one of those 'happy to be alive' moments!" Get the difference?

So my description of a highlight may be inspiring, but why would my wife and I also share our lowlight? That seems like a drag. There's something about human nature that forges a powerful bond in adversity. One of our ministers used to joke about the difference between how men and women communicate. Two men will meet for the first time, pretend that everything in their lives is going great, and talk about sports. Two women will meet, and the dialogue might go like this:

"I just broke a heel on my favorite shoes running over here in the rain."

"I've been there. Let me tell you where I get fabulous bargains on shoes...."

Those women have formed a much stronger bond in sharing their adversity than the men who pretend they have no problems. It's the same process in sharing my lowlights with my wife. Her role is to listen without trying to fix anything. All I want is to be heard. And it feels great to know your partner knows what's really going on in your life, so you don't feel so isolated and alone.

Again, the idea is to capture a moment in time. "I had a crummy day at work today," is not nearly as captivating as, "When I went in to check out a laptop and projector for my presentation, the receptionist grilled me about how long I'd keep it, as if I were some kind of selfish jerk who hogged everything for myself. It really ticked me off."

Who hasn't had that kind of moment, when a little thing in your day *really* sends you through the roof, but you just let it go because life is just too short? Bringing those moments back with your spouse allows her to know what's really going on in your head, and it feels good to commiserate. It's as if you're both acknowledging that "Yeah, life is hard, and we suffer a lot in our daily travails. But ain't it great that we've got a friend who feels the same way?" It's also an excellent way to notice and manage the anxiety that instantly wells up inside you when your spouse shares his pain. The goal is to avoid taking on his anxiety and to avoid trying to fix it for him. Just to be present to his anxiety is more than enough. We think of it as "letting some air out of the balloon of our anxiety": things are not quite so amorphous and scary once you articulate them.

If you try this highlight/lowlight with your spouse at dinner, you'll be surprised how it instantly pulls you both together and gives you a sense of shared intimacy.[2] Nothing lights up our family's meals together like sharing the best and worst moments of our day. If you're worried about your worst moment being a downer for the rest of the meal, share it first. That way, you can "cancel out" its effects by sharing your highlight immediately afterward. Also, when your low-light is a little too grim to share in front of the kids, you can always discuss it later.

## The Shortcut to Marital Bliss:
## Visit Your Parents

Everyone likes a shortcut. People often ask me for a "technique" they can apply to improve their marriage and parenting. Well, here it is:

As I hinted in chapters 7 and 9, the best thing you can do for your marriage and your kids is to visit your parents for at least one weekend every three months (preferably alone). Confide in them about what's really going on in your life. And earn their trust, so that they confide about their lives to you. The best thing you can do for your children, and for your own life trajectory, is to spend more time with your parents. Not just "face time," where everyone's polite but distant, but actual *quality* time.

Before you recoil in horror at spending all that precious time with Mom and Dad, let me explain what's in it for you. What you resist persists. What you distance from, ignore, or pretend doesn't matter will persist. Simply being in contact with our parents reduces our anxiety in life. I even know a physician who claims that repairing her cut-off from her family actually healed her chronic depression.

Your goal is to complete your Incomplete Weaning from your parents. This doesn't mean tearing yourself away roughly, like most of us do. I also don't mean going to the other extreme, where we continue to act like children, being coddled and taken care of by our parents. That's not growing up either.

It means gently gaining our independence from them, while staying in close contact. It's about becoming an equal with our parents. Using them as a resource of valuable advice — not a crutch to rescue us or hover over us.

The transition of our relationship from parent-child to equals is sure to be bumpy along the way, and you can expect some drama and conflict. Certain things are hard to change. Don't fight your anger. If you notice it and accept it, it lessens. Learning to observe your anxiety inside you calms you down, and the calmer you are the easier it is to observe yourself. So the glass is half full. If you're noticing you're anxious, that's great! It means you're less anxious than back in the days when you were so anxious you couldn't even tell you were; it just seemed like everyone else was on your case.

But the payoff is huge, in that the more we gently complete our weaning from our parents, the less anxiety we will carry into our relationships with spouse and kids. That means we'll be less judgmental of ourselves and others. We can bring more objectivity to the problems that pop up in life. When we attach less drama to a problem, it makes us more thoughtful and resourceful in problem solving.

That's why working on our relationship with our parents has a ripple effect throughout all our relationships. If you can go back to the source, the herd whose imprinting gave you those reactivity patterns, and change those patterns within your original herd, those patterns will change in all your subsequent relationships as well.

For example, Scott in chapter 7 improved his weaning from his mother in Maine, and his wife tells me how he's now slower to overreact in their marriage. Cynthia's safari work in her family of origin gave her the courage to better stand up for herself, so she could forge a more equal partnership in her marriage. She no longer felt taken advantage of by her husband, which increased her long-term fulfillment in her marriage and warded off any threat of divorce.

## Where Do We Go from Here?

Now that we've finished this book, we have to go build a dependable friendship with our spouse, but we cannot minimize the challenges we face.

There's still plenty of anxiety filling up the pot of our marriage, and sometimes it's going to boil over. We're going to blame our spouses (and vice versa), we're going to distance from our spouses (and vice versa), and we're going to project our anxiety onto our children via attunement. How can we manage our anxiety so that those patterns are less harmful to our marriage and our kids?

Here's the thing I want most for you to take away from this book:

We need to remove all the exits from our marriage. We all married someone at the same level of anxiety. We are not superior to our spouses. We cannot look down on them.

But we can learn compassion: our spouse is just doing the best he can, given the hand he was dealt.

And it's humbling to realize just how much our anxiety runs our behavior. We, too, are just doing the best we can, given the hand we were dealt.

So let's always remember that, of our three options for boiling pots, it's much better to argue and blame than to distance or project onto our kids. Direct emotional engagement is the best option. Even the happiest couples have chronic arguments that never get resolved.

And direct, emotional engagement is *exciting*. When you give up the myth that arguing equals divorce, then an argument is just blowing off steam. And emotional engagement on our walks, whether we're arguing or sharing our thoughts, feelings, and dreams, is exciting. Being in motion with our emotions feels more dynamic and alive than sitting down in the living room to have a "serious" conversation. It's also emotional engagement that breathes new joy into our sex life and renews the physical intimacy to accompany our newfound emotional intimacy.

So *that's* where we go from here. We've already married our ideal mate, with our same level of anxiety, and now it's up to each of us to notice and manage that anxiety. But how do we do that?

I once attended a seminar on communication in marriage and was deeply moved by a presentation. Afterward I went up and asked the speaker how to become a better listener. He replied, "The best way to become a better listener is to notice when you're not."

This book offers a few ways to create a better family, but it's more about not harming the family we already have. I imagine at times you have felt overwhelmed by all this talk about Blaming Our Spouse, Distancing from Our Spouse, and Projecting onto Our Children. Learning what *not* to do may seem like a negative message, but in many ways I think it's easier (and more effective) than if I handed you a to-do list of new tasks. All we have to do is become aware of what we're *already* doing, all day, every day. As soon as we become aware, we'll engage in fewer of these negative behaviors because it's so obviously in our self-interest not to engage in them.

So let me reassure you about a few things.

First, you don't have to be perfect. None of us ever will be, because imperfection is the human condition. Perfection is not the goal; progress is. You start wherever you are, and you strive to become a little more self-aware and make some progress in monitoring and managing your anxiety. Sure, some folks around you are less anxious than you, and their lives go more smoothly. But you know what? Other folks around you are more anxious, and they encounter even *more* drama and heartache in their lives. So you see, it doesn't matter where you start. It just matters that you commit to your marriage and make *progress*.

Remember the metaphor about the ship's captain who had mapped out the route for his ship's journey? Before you became aware of your anxiety, blame, distancing, and projection, you already had a predetermined route picked out for your ship. You didn't choose your ship's route, your level of anxiety did.

But now that you're aware of your anxiety you can alter your ship's journey and avoid some rough seas. Not a lot, maybe just 1 percent. But what a difference that 1 percent can make! Perhaps you're an anxious type, so your marriage was destined to go bad. But now, thanks to your 1 percent increased self-awareness, your marriage will go less badly than it was originally routed to go. Perhaps that will be enough to keep your marriage intact, whereas you might otherwise have ended up divorced. Perhaps you made enough progress so that you didn't have to start over again with someone else. That's real progress!

The other good news about becoming self-aware of your anxiety is that you don't have to change anybody else. You don't have to fix everyone around you in order to be content. You don't have to wait until everyone's nice before you can be happy. *You* have the power to control your destiny.

We all know what a dead-end it is to try to change our loved ones, right? Indeed, marriage is *not* a correctional institution. So there's tremendous relief in knowing that *we* have control of our lives; it's up to us how much progress we make, and we no longer feel tossed around on the stormy seas of fate. We have a say in how we do, and how our children do. And it's never too late to do better — to improve, to make progress.

Another wonderful thing about self-awareness of your anxiety is that it gives you *compassion*. Now you understand how every single person you meet is *up against it*. They're struggling with the same anxiety, the same demons in their heads, that you struggle with. We spend most of the day, every day, *overreacting* to each other. And most folks out there don't even *realize* that's what they're doing, and they *certainly* have no idea how to change it. That's why they seek solace in medication, alcohol, or an affair. They desperately want relief, but don't know how to get it.

But *you* know. It's a lifelong process, but at least now you have a clear route, one that you chose yourself. You know that your ticket to relief is to increasingly notice and control your anxiety as much as possible as you interact with your parents and siblings. From now on, you have a direction, and you no longer have to learn from trial and error. You know that every ounce of effort you put toward this goal will pay dividends and have a ripple effect through all your relationships. How's *that* for motivation? You'll no longer be flailing in the dark, hoping things get better, or at least, don't get worse. You now know how to make slow, steady progress. And slow, steady progress is exactly what I wish for you.

I'd love to hear from you as soon as you close this book. You can reach me at *david@DavidArthurCode.com*. I'm interested in hearing your stories, which points resonated most strongly with you, and what your plans are for applying the lessons of this book in your own family. Thank you for joining me on this bold, hopeful journey, and here's to 1 percent of progress and a new course for your ship!

# Notes

Introduction

    1. Kate Stone Lombardi, "Helping Clergy Help the Anguished," *New York Times,* April 2, 2000.

    2. John Gottman, *What Predicts Divorce: The Relationship between Marital Processes and Marital Outcomes* (Hillsdale, N.J.: Lawrence Erlbaum Associates, 1993).

    3. David Popenoe with the National Marriage Project at Rutgers University and the 2006 American Community Survey for Bexar County. Jennifer Baker's statistics are even higher, as cited by Andrew Herrmann: "To Have and to Hold," *Chicago Sun-Times,* June 9, 2003.

Chapter 1 / How We Create a Self-Fulfilling Prophecy in Our Kids

    1. Murray Bowen, *Family Therapy in Clinical Practice* (Northvale, N.J.: Jason Aronson Press, 1978), 21, 27.

    2. Richard Charles wrote in the *American Journal of Family Therapy* that "Bowen's theory that parents of schizophrenics were more fused with their offspring than were other parents was also confirmed"; see L. Wichstrom and A. Holte, "Fusion in the Parent Relationships of Schizophrenics," *Psychiatry* 58 (1993): 28–43.

    3. "The Top 10: The Most Influential Therapists of the Past Quarter-Century," *Psychotherapy Networker* (March–April 2007).

    4. Judith Warner, *Perfect Madness: Motherhood in the Age of Anxiety* (New York: Riverhead Books, 2005), 133.

    5. Madeline Levine, *The Price of Privilege: How Parental Pressure and Material Advantage Are Creating a Generation of Disconnected and Unhappy Kids* (New York: HarperCollins, 2006), 141.

    6. Warner, *Perfect Madness,* 55.

7. Michael Kerr, *Family Evaluation: An Approach Based on Bowen Theory* (New York: W. W. Norton, 1988), 182.

8. Science reporter Daniel Goleman interviewed John Cacioppo for the *New York Times,* December 15, 1992, and cites his personal notes from that interview in *Emotional Intelligence* (New York: Bantam, 1995), 179. Goleman also addresses this topic in the flap copy for *Social Intelligence: The New Science of Human Relationships* (New York: Bantam, 2006): "It's [a] most fundamental discovery: we are designed for sociability, constantly engaged in a 'neural ballet' that connects us brain to brain with those around us. Our reactions to others, and theirs to us, have a far-reaching biological impact, sending out cascades of hormones that regulate everything from our hearts to our immune systems, making good relationships act like vitamins — and bad relationships like poisons. We can 'catch' other people's emotions the way we catch a cold."

9. Kerr, *Family Evaluation,* 200–201.

10. Ibid., 182.

11. Ibid., 7.

12. Levine, *The Price of Privilege,* 140–41.

13. Nicholas Wade, "Genes Show Limited Value in Predicting Diseases," *New York Times,* April 16, 2009.

14. Michael Kerr, "Why Do Siblings Turn Out So Differently?" available online from the Bowen Center.

15. Sarah Hrdy, *Mother Nature: A History of Mothers, Infants, and Natural Selection* (New York: Pantheon, 1999), 72. Hrdy lays to rest the extremely popular misconception that most ailments are "genetic." She distinguishes between genes and "epigenetics," which means the influence of the environment on a gene. All humans can do is pass on a genetic predisposition for an ailment. It is the epigenetics, the influence of the environment (which includes family dynamics), that determines whether that genetic predisposition will actually be manifest as an ailment or not. One gene can produce many different "phenotypes," or manifestations, depending on its environment: "The identical genotype (or at least genotypes that are very similar, as in full siblings) could develop

into an organism that looks or behaves very differently (that is, exhibits a different phenotype). . . . Long overlooked, polyphenism, the outcome of so many underlying mysteries, is assuming greater importance in the thinking of geneticists. Anyone tempted by cascading research that identifies genes 'for' particular traits would do well to keep these cases in mind, as reminders of how much context still matters" (72).

16. Goleman, *Social Intelligence*, 156 and 226.

17. If you search online at the National Library of Medicine, you will find more than three hundred medical articles on Fetal (or Prenatal) Programming. See *www.PubMed.gov*.

18. W. Schlotz, "Fetal Origins of Mental Health: Evidence and Mechanisms," *Brain, Behavior and Immunity,* Epub: February 13, 2009.

19. T. Berry Brazelton, "Family Pattern Stirs Concern about Over-Mothered Child," *Albany Times Union,* August 29, 2007: "The problem with an 'over-mothered' child is well known in pediatrics, where it is sometimes called the 'Vulnerable Child Syndrome.' Overprotection affects the child's image of himself, leaving him to feel that he always needs to be protected, and that he is unable to take care of himself. . . . We see this in mothers who are having a lonely, tough time themselves."

20. Goleman, *Social Intelligence,* 224.

21. For a discussion of "idiopathic" autism, which is stable over time, versus "secondary" autism, which is rapidly increasing, see Joseph D. Buxbaum, "The Genetics of Autism Spectrum Disorders," *Medscape Psychiatry and Mental Health* 10, no. 2 (2005).

22. Jon Hamilton, "Cyber Scout Puts Autism Studies on Faster Track," *Morning Edition,* National Public Radio, April 8, 2009.

23. John D. Kelly, M.D., "Marriage: Your Life Depends on It," *Orthopedics Today* (April 2009). The research of doctors Bowen, Sherry, Kerr, and others also suggests that a distant marriage could contribute to the high anxiety levels of these mothers.

24. Susan Dominus, "The Allergy Prison," *New York Times Magazine,* June 10, 2001, 63.

25. Jaak Panksepp, *Affective Neuroscience: The Foundations of Human and Animal Emotions* (New York: Oxford University Press, 1998), 320.

26. Stephanie Coontz, "Till Children Do Us Part," *New York Times,* February 5, 2009.

27. Sue Shellenbarger, "Helicopter Parenting: A Breakdown," *Wall Street Journal,* September 27, 2007.

28. Benjamin Spock, "Russian Children Don't Whine, Squabble or Break Things — Why?" *Ladies Home Journal* (October 1960): "Parents who lacked confidence in their own common sense became anxious about the possible harm they might do their children if they inhibited them or made them resentful through discipline. . . . They decided when in doubt it was better not to interfere. . . . Their children have felt a lack of direction, and often acted up. The parents have tried hard to suppress their irritation at the misbehavior. But each time their patience has broken they have felt guilty and tried harder to suppress the irritation. I think that this kind of conflict in parents — between irritation and guilt — is what has allowed a lot, not all, of the minor squabbling, whining, inconsiderateness, abuse of toys and furnishings which are so common in American children."

29. David Sherry, "Psychosomatic Musculoskeletal Pain in Childhood: Clinical and Psychological Analyses of 100 Children" *Pediatrics* 88, no. 6 (December 1991): 1093–99; M. D. Klinnert et al., "Onset and Persistence of Childhood Asthma: Predictors from Infancy" *Pediatrics* 108, no. 4 (October 2001): e69.

30. Warner, *Perfect Madness,* 133.

## Chapter 2 / Why We Kill Our Kids with Kindness

1. Dr. Michael Kerr is an author and psychiatrist with extensive research and counseling experience at the Georgetown Family Center in Washington, D.C. This example is a composite of a case study that Dr. Kerr describes as typical, combined with a story from my personal observation. Michael Kerr, *Family Evaluation:*

*An Approach Based on Bowen Theory* (New York: W. W. Norton, 1988), 204–5.

2. Jaak Panksepp, *Affective Neuroscience: The Foundations of Human and Animal Emotions* (New York: Oxford University Press, 1998), 21.

3. Sarah Hrdy, *Mother Nature: A History of Mothers, Infants, and Natural Selection* (New York: Pantheon, 1999), 153–54.

4. Jack Nitschke et al., "Orbitofrontal Cortex Tracks Positive Mood in Mothers Viewing Pictures of Their Newborn Infants," *NeuroImage* 21 (2004): 583–92.

5. Daniel Goleman, *Social Intelligence: The New Science of Human Relationships* (New York: Bantam, 2006), 215.

6. Hrdy, *Mother Nature*, 536.

7. Daniel Stern, *The Interpersonal World of the Infant* (New York: Basic Books, 1987), 30.

8. Hrdy, *Mother Nature*, 379.

9. Ibid., 388.

10. Madeline Levine, *The Price of Privilege: How Parental Pressure and Material Advantage Are Creating a Generation of Disconnected and Unhappy Kids* (New York: HarperCollins, 2006), 141.

11. Goleman, *Social Intelligence*, 164.

12. *janegoodall.org/chimp_central/chimpanzees/f_family/flo.asp.*

13. Goleman, *Social Intelligence*, 193.

14. Kerr, *Family Evaluation*, 7.

15. Ibid., 116.

16. Ibid., 198–99.

17. Panksepp, *Affective Neuroscience*, 225–47.

18. Goleman, *Emotional Intelligence*, 100: Cornell psychiatrist Daniel Stern provides us with a great example of the subtle, insidious ways that a well-intentioned mother projects her anxiety about her marriage with her husband onto one of her newborn twins, thereby creating two very different personalities, as described by Daniel Goleman (emphasis added): "Sarah was twenty-five when she gave birth to twin boys, Mark and Fred. Mark, she felt, was more like herself; Fred was more like his father. That perception

may have been the seed of a telling but subtle difference in how she treated each boy. When the boys were just three months old, Sarah would often try to catch Fred's gaze, and when he would avert his face, she would try to catch his eye again; Fred would respond by turning away more emphatically. Once she would look away, Fred would look back at her, and the cycle of pursuit and aversion would begin again — often leaving Fred in tears. But with Mark, Sarah virtually never tried to impose eye contact as she did with Fred. Instead Mark could break off eye contact whenever he wanted, and she would not pursue.

"A small act, but telling. A year later, Fred was noticeably more fearful and dependent than Mark; one way he showed his fearfulness was by breaking off eye contact with other people, as he had done with his mother at three months, turning his face down and away. Mark, on the other hand, looked people straight in the eye; when he wanted to break off contact, he'd turn his head slightly upward and to the side, with a winning smile.

"The twins and their mother were observed minutely when they took part in research by Daniel Stern, a psychiatrist then at Cornell University School of Medicine. Stern is fascinated by the small, repeated exchanges that take place between parent and child; he believes that the most basic lessons of emotional life are laid down in these intimate moments. Of all such moments, the most critical are those that let the child know her emotions are met with empathy, accepted, and reciprocated, in a process Stern calls attunement. The twins' mother was attuned with Mark, but out of emotional synch with Fred. Stern contends that the countlessly repeated moments of attunement or misattunement between parent and child shape the emotional expectations adults bring to their close relationships — perhaps far more than the more dramatic events of childhood."

19. Ibid., 22.
20. Ibid., 181–82.
21. Goodall as cited in Hrdy, *Mother Nature,* 89.
22. Kerr, *Family Evaluation,* 96–97.

23. Goleman, *Social Intelligence,* 215, 204.

24. Ibid., 14.

25. Ibid., 195. Goleman nicely paraphrases Cassidy and Shaver's studies of these anxious types in romantic relationships. See also Jude Cassidy and Phillip Shaver, eds., *Handbook of Attachment Theory: Research and Clinical Applications* (New York: Guilford Press, 1999).

26. Goleman, *Social Intelligence,* 183.

27. The Pulitzer Prize columnist Colbert King asserts in the *Washington Post* that discrimination and ailing school systems are merely symptoms, not the cause of our kids' problems: "Fix the family. Anything less, political rhetoric notwithstanding, and we'll just keep fussing about the schools, inventing new Band-Aid programs and digging those burial plots." Colbert King, "The Breakdown That Really Needs Fixing," *Washington Post,* December 9, 2006.

## Chapter 3 / Why We Hurt Those We Love Most

1. Daniel Goleman, *Emotional Intelligence* (New York: Bantam, 1995), 60.

2. Ibid., 135.

3. Michael Kerr, *Family Evaluation: An Approach Based on Bowen Theory* (New York: W. W. Norton, 1988), 187.

4. Jaak Panksepp, *Affective Neuroscience: The Foundations of Human and Animal Emotions* (New York: Oxford University Press, 1998), 189.

5. Frans de Waal, *Our Inner Ape: A Leading Primatologist Explains Why We Are Who We Are* (New York: Riverhead Books, 2005), 162.

6. Ibid., 163.

7. Cited in Goleman, *Emotional Intelligence,* 59.

8. de Waal, *Our Inner Ape,* 164.

9. Kerr, *Family Evaluation,* 187.

10. Ibid., 190.

## Chapter 4 / The Silent Killer of Marriage

1. Daniel Goleman, *Emotional Intelligence* (New York: Bantam, 1995), 136.

2. Katie Hafner, "Laptop Slides into Bed in Love Triangle," *New York Times,* August 24, 2006.

3. Madeline Levine, *The Price of Privilege: How Parental Pressure and Material Advantage Are Creating a Generation of Disconnected and Unhappy Kids* (New York: HarperCollins, 2006), 31.

4. There is an excellent book on this topic by Peter Titelman, ed., *Emotional Cutoff: Bowen Family Systems Theory Perspectives* (New York: Haworth, 2003).

5. Michael Kerr, *Family Evaluation: An Approach Based on Bowen Theory* (New York: W. W. Norton, 1988), 272.

6. Ibid., 137.

7. Murray Bowen, *Family Therapy in Clinical Practice* (Northvale, N.J.: Jason Aronson Press, 1978), 54.

8. Ibid., 38.

## Chapter 5 / Anxiety: The Cause of Drama in Relationships

1. Daniel Goleman, *Emotional Intelligence* (New York: Bantam, 1995), 5.

2. Ibid., 17.

3. Daniel Goleman, *Social Intelligence: The New Science of Human Relationships* (New York: Bantam, 2006), 268.

4. Goleman, *Emotional Intelligence,* 5.

5. Marc Siegel, "The Irony of Fear: Irrational Health Anxieties Boost Your Risk of the Conditions You Should Fear the Most," *Washington Post,* August 30, 2005.

6. Nicholas Wade, "Pas de Deux of Sexuality Is Written in the Genes," *New York Times,* April 10, 2007.

7. Jaak Panksepp, *Affective Neuroscience: The Foundations of Human and Animal Emotions* (New York: Oxford University Press, 1998), 72.

8. Goleman, *Emotional Intelligence,* 24.

9. Goleman, *Social Intelligence,* 225.

10. Michael Kerr, *Family Evaluation: An Approach Based on Bowen Theory* (New York: W. W. Norton, 1988), 336–37.

11. Goleman, *Social Intelligence*, 174.

12. Ibid., 42.

13. Frans de Waal, *Our Inner Ape: A Leading Primatologist Explains Why We Are Who We Are* (New York: Bantam, 2005), 178–79.

## Chapter 6 / The Grass Is Not Greener: You've Already Chosen Your Ideal Mate

1. S. Ortigue and F. Bianchi-Demicheli, "Why Is Your Spouse So Predictable? Connecting Mirror Neuron System and Self-Expansion Model of Love," *Medical Hypotheses* 71, no. 6 (December 2008): 941–44. Epub: August 21, 2008.

2. Michael Kerr observes that "many people who have been divorced have a firm determination to keep a subsequent marriage intact," in Michael Kerr, *Family Evaluation: An Approach Based on Bowen Theory* (New York: W. W. Norton, 1988), 295.

3. David Popenoe with the National Marriage Project at Rutgers University and the 2006 American Community Survey for Bexar County. Jennifer Baker's statistics are even higher, as cited by Andrew Herrmann in "To Have and to Hold," *Chicago Sun-Times,* June 9, 2003.

4. Jaak Panksepp, *Affective Neuroscience: The Foundations of Human and Animal Emotions* (New York: Oxford University Press, 1998), 21.

5. Helen Fisher, "Romantic Love: A Mammalian Brain System for Mate Choice," *Philosophical Transactions of the Royal Society of London* 361, no. 1476 (December 2006): 2173–86.

6. Daniel Goleman, *Social Intelligence: The New Science of Human Relationships* (New York: Bantam, 2006), 198.

7. Melissa Curan, "How Representations of the Parental Marriage Predict Marital Emotional Attunement During the Transition to Parenthood," *Journal of Family Psychology* 20, no. 3 (2006): 477–84.

8. S. Zeki, "The Neurobiology of Love," *FEBS Letters* 581, no. 14 (June 12, 2007): 2575–79. Epub: May 8, 2007.

9. Goleman, *Social Intelligence,* 5.

10. Frans de Waal, *Our Inner Ape: A Leading Primatologist Explains Why We Are Who We Are* (New York: Bantam, 2005), 107–8.

11. "Anthropologists refer to this tendency to be drawn to some-one like yourself 'positive assortive mating' or 'fitness matching,' " writes Helen Fisher in *Why We Love: The Nature and Chemistry of Romantic Love* (New York: Henry Holt, 2004), 103.

12. Ibid., 144.

13. J. F. Lepage, "The Mirror Neuron System: Grasping Others' Actions from Birth?" *Developmental Science* 10, no. 5 (September 2007): 513–23.

14. de Waal, *Our Inner Ape,* 179.

15. The late Dr. Murray Bowen and his colleague Dr. Michael Kerr are considered the leading proponents of this theory, and Bowen is rated the seventh most influential psychiatrist in the past twenty-five years by *Psychotherapy Networker* magazine. Professor Martin Rovers confirms in his research that we choose mates with the same level of anxiety as we have (Rovers uses the term "differentiation" to mean level of anxiety): "This research gives strong support and credence to Bowen's premise that people get engaged to and marry a partner of equal differentiation [i.e., anxiety] when defined in a similar and complementary manner. The results indicated that 66.7 percent of those couples tested choose partners of equal differentiation and/or undifferentiation" (Martin Rovers et al., "Choosing a Partner of Equal Differentiation: A New Paradigm Utilizing Similarity and Complementarity Measures," *Journal of Couple and Relationship Therapy* 6, no. 3 [November 2007]: 1–23).

16. Sarah Hrdy, *Mother Nature: A History of Mothers, Infants, and Natural Selection* (New York: Pantheon, 1999), 245, quoting from David M. Buss et al., "International Preferences in Selecting Mates: A Study of 37 Cultures," *Journal of Cross-Cultural Psychology* 21 (1992): 5–47.

17. Michael Kerr, *Family Evaluation: An Approach Based on Bowen Theory* (New York: W. W. Norton, 1988), 167.

18. Ibid., 171: "High energy people often marry low energy people, 'cyclic' people marry 'steady' people, and people who are calm on the surface often marry flamboyant people. This can occur even when people are determined to create a family situation that is different from (better than) the one in which they grew up. The repetition of the past in spite of the determination to do otherwise is a product of people's efforts being based on false assumptions about the nature of the problems in their original family. People can change the superficial appearance of things through efforts based on false assumptions, but underlying processes are not altered. One purpose of therapy is to question the accuracy of assumptions about past generations and in the process to develop a more reliable blueprint for directing one's efforts with present and future generations."

19. Cheryl Lavin, "It's True: Bad Boys Get Good Girls," *Chicago Tribune,* June 11, 2004.

### Chapter 7 / Take a Crash Course on Your Family's History So You Don't Repeat It

1. Michael Kerr, *Family Evaluation: An Approach Based on Bowen Theory* (New York: W. W. Norton, 1988), 213.

### Chapter 8 / To Fix Your Child's Problem, Fix It in Yourself First

1. Carl Jung, "The Development of the Personality" (1934), in *Collected Works* 17: *The Development of the Personality,* 287.

2. Murray Bowen's "Bowen Family Systems Theory" gives us an excellent framework through which to view relationships and self-fulfilling prophecies. See Murray Bowen, *Family Therapy in Clinical Practice* (Northvale, N.J.: Jason Aronson Press, 1978).

### Chapter 9 / We Get So Much Good Advice, but Why Can't We Follow Through?

1. Robert Pear, "Married and Single Parents Spending More Time with Children, Study Finds," *New York Times,* October 17, 2006.

2. David Hochman, "Mommy (and Me)," *New York Times,* January 30, 2005.

3. Gina Piccalo quotes Judith Warner, author of *A Perfect Madness: Motherhood in the Age of Anxiety*, in "It Takes a Guru, a Pricey Pram and a Village," *Los Angeles Times,* June 18, 2006.

4. Murray Bowen, *Family Therapy in Clinical Practice* (Northvale, N.J.: Jason Aronson Press, 1978), 216.

5. Although Vic and Kendra were trying a method they had heard about by word-of-mouth, it bears similarities to the Ferber Method.

6. Daniel Goleman, *Social Intelligence: The New Science of Human Relationships* (New York: Bantam, 2006), 184.

## Chapter 10 / Eat, Walk, and Talk Your Way to a Happier Family

1. Murray Bowen, *Family Therapy in Clinical Practice* (Northvale, N.J.: Jason Aronson Press, 1978).

2. Although I have never read their book, I am told Dennis, Sheila, and Matthew Linn offer similar advice in *Good Goats: Healing Our Image of God* (Mahwah, N.J.: Paulist Press, 1993).

# *Of Related Interest*

David Robinson
**THE BUSY FAMILY'S GUIDE
TO SPIRITUALITY**
*Practical Lessons for Modern Living
from the Monastic Tradition*

"The most innovative book I have seen in family spirituality." —*Spiritual Life*

Drawing on timeless principles of monastic communal living, this spiritual guide for families offers effective tools to meet today's challenges and counteract the divisive forces that can splinter a healthy home. Written by a pastor who is a father of three grown sons and Benedictine Oblate of Mount Angel Abbey, this book includes dozens of practical suggestions and exercises based on the Benedictine monastic tradition.

978-0-8245-2524-8, paperback

# *Of Related Interest*

**Keith W. Frome, Ed.D.**
**WHAT NOT TO EXPECT**
*A Meditation on the Spirituality of Parenting*

Winner of the First Place
Catholic Press Award for Parenting

The multi-million-selling series *What to Expect When You're Expecting* tries to take the guesswork and fear out of being a parent by offering parents checklists, tips, and timelines for how to know what's coming next in a child's life.

Dr. Keith Frome admits that he and his wife love the *What to Expect* series. But as a professional educator, headmaster of a K-8 private school, and parent of two boys, he sees every day how children surprise us, frustrate us, and simply refuse to follow the checklist we prepared for them.

Dr. Frome takes us through dozens of things families experience every day — winning and losing, eating, falling down, pooping — and shows how each of these catch us offguard.

0-8245-2282-6, paperback

## *Of Related Interest*

**Keith Frome, Ed.D.**
**HOW'S MY KID DOING**
*Practical Answers to Questions*
*about Your Child's Education*

*Foreword Magazine* Medal Winner!

"Frome combines two decades of concrete experience with a warmth and wisdom that help you
understand your kid, your school, and yourself
more clearly than ever."
— **Kinney Zalesne,** coauthor, *Microtrends:*
*The Small Forces Behind Tomorrow's Big Changes*

While children are known for asking tough questions wherever they go, their parents often feel
left alone with the overwhelming challenges of
education in today's complex world. Longtime
headmaster and educator Keith Frome has lis-
tened to parents for years. In this helpful book he
gathers sound, practical advice on a multitude of
parents' most pressing questions along with the
latest research and trends regarding homework,
curriculum, discipline, and social and moral issues.

A rare and valuable resource for every parent of a
child K-12.

978-0-8245-2424-1, paperback

# Of Related Interest

**Tian Dayton, Ph.D.**
**MODERN MOTHERING**
*How to Teach Kids to Say What They Feel*
*and Feel What They Say*

From her appearances on Oprah to her role as a mother, professor, and counselor, Tian Dayton helps us to see the importance of the mother-child relationship. How do children actually learn to articulate their emotional needs? Dr. Dayton offers a remarkable solution, showing how mothers can guide their children to emotional literacy in order to find their true selves, express creativity, and lead productive lives.

0-8245-2340-7, paperback

Check your local bookstore for availability.
To order directly from the publisher,
please call 1-800-888-4741 for Customer Service
or visit our website at *www.cpcbooks.com.*

**31901046477677**